Praise for *Worms at Work*

This isn't just a book about vermicomposting (although it does
a great job teaching the how and why), it is a book that tells the magical
story of how soil is a whole world of microorganism and organic matter
below our feet and can be regenerated to create fertility in the garden and
sequester carbon on the planet for the health of all species. This is at
the cutting edge of permaculture thinking and research, admirably
explained and with a host of great illustrations and photographs.

MADDY HARLAND Editor and Co-Founder,
Permaculture Magazine

Worms at Work is a great starting point for exploring the basics
of soil science and composting. Unlike a lot of other books on soil, this
book is easily digestible; readable in a weekend and written for students
and beginning gardeners. Overall, Crystal Stevens does an excellent job of
combining soil theory with practical, hands on ways to learn more and to start
building soil with worms today — no land or fancy equipment required.
While the book is readable for a weekend, there are weeks worth of
activities in the book to bring the learning to life. If I wanted to get
someone excited about soil, this is the book I would give them.

DIEGO FOOTER author *Bokashi Composting*

Reading this engaging and practical guide by Crystal Stevens will
surely turn anyone into an earthworm enthusiast. After chapters devoted to
earthworm biology and their role in building healthy soil, she provides easy-
to-follow instructions for raising worms on any scale, from small kitchen bins
to backyard compost piles and ingeniously designed worm farms. She even
includes ideas for earthworm field days and school lessons to spread the
love of these amazing creatures in the community. A great little guide
to everything you need to know about earthworms!

LINDA GILKESON author, *Backyard Bounty*

Worms at Work is a detailed, beautifully thorough treatise on worms. It delves into the details of vermicomposting, how to skillfully utilize vermicompost, the soil science behind it all, worm anatomy, and much more. It is well organized and easy to reference - perfect for anyone wanting to start or refine the usage of worms in a home or garden situation. Following in the footsteps of Darwin with her praise of the mighty earthworm, Crystal Stevens has done a superb job with this much-needed and timely work.

MATT POWERS educator and author, *The Permaculture Student Series*, ThePermacultureStudent.com

Humans seem to have a relationship with worms that goes beyond mere curiosity. We all emerge from a worm of sperm and return to the embrace of worms recycling our remains. They start us, they complete us. In *Worms at Work*, Crystal Stevens opens the bigger can, asking: "what if big companies, factories, and corporations simply stopped producing anything made from nonrenewable resources and instead made the same items from renewable resources such as agricultural waste, hemp, and bamboo?" Worms could save our civilization.

ALBERT BATES author, *The Post-Petroleum Survival Guide*, *The Biochar Solution*, and *The Paris Agreement*

Crystal Stevens combines years of experience with her love of teaching to present a straightforward and gentle introduction to raising beneficial worms. Her passion for sustainable living and organic gardening rings true with her ideas for how homesteaders and worms can team up to create a better world – both above and below-ground.

HANNAH KINCAID, *Mother Earth News*

Worms
AT WORK

Worms
AT WORK

CRYSTAL STEVENS

HARNESSING THE AWESOME POWER OF WORMS WITH VERMICULTURE AND VERMICOMPOSTING

new society
PUBLISHERS

Cover design by Diane McIntosh.
Cover and all interior photos by Crystal Stevens unless otherwise noted.

Printed in Canada. Second Printing, January 2021.

Inquiries regarding requests to reprint all or part of *Worms at Work* should be addressed to New Society Publishers at the address below. To order directly from the publishers, please call toll-free (North America) 1-800-567-6772, or order online at www.newsociety.com

Any other inquiries can be directed by mail to:
New Society Publishers
P.O. Box 189, Gabriola Island, BC V0R 1X0, Canada
(250) 247-9737

LIBRARY AND ARCHIVES CANADA CATALOGUING IN PUBLICATION

Stevens, Crystal J., author
    Worms at work : harnessing the awesome power of worms
with vermiculture and vermicomposting I Crystal Stevens.

Issued in print and electronic formats.
ISBN 978-0-86571-840-1 (softcover).--ISBN 978-1-55092-635-4 (PDF).
--ISBN 978-1-77142-229-1 (EPUB)

    1. Earthworm culture--Handbooks, manuals, etc. 2.
Vermicomposting-Handbooks, manuals, etc. I. Title.

SF597.E3S74 2017   639'.75   C2017-902648-8   C2017-902649-6

Funded by the Government of Canada	Financé par le gouvernement du Canada	Canada

New Society Publishers' mission is to publish books that contribute in fundamental ways to building an ecologically sustainable and just society, and to do so with the least possible impact on the environment, in a manner that models this vision.

CONTENTS

INTRODUCTION

WORMS AT WORK discusses the vital role most worms play in soil health, soil fertility, and the longevity of ecosystems. It encompasses the important roles worms play in food production and the reasons every gardener should have both a compost bin and a vermicompost bin to help increase resilience and decrease reliance on toxic synthetic fertilizers. It also discusses the aspect of low- to no-budget gardening. *Worms at Work* gives practical instruction on how to create and maintain a home or school vermicompost bin, including a plethora of resources in the form of worksheets, lesson plans, observation records, coloring sheets, and a whole slew of activities revolving around the worm bin that could integrate vermiculture into the science curriculum in both the classroom and homeschool setting. It also provides detailed instruction on how to build and maintain vermicomposting bins for the backyard setting. It discusses how to harvest and store worm castings and the various garden applications in which worm castings could benefit plant growth and health. Chapter 8 discusses how to share worms and knowledge for the greater good of the community.

Vermicomposting and organic gardening go hand in hand. Organic is better for the environment! Humans had been growing organically up until the 20th century, when chemicals developed in the wake of the two world wars led to the "Green Revolution." The

Green Revolution was not actually very green, and unfortunately these new growing methods, which quickly became the norm in industrialized nations worldwide, led to a devastating loss of healthy topsoil that had been built up over millennia. Pesticides, herbicides, and fungicides (etc.) contaminate our groundwater with toxins that are harmful to the soil, the water, and our bodies, especially for children who are particularly vulnerable to toxic exposures.

The Earth's surface is composed of approximately 30% land and 70% water. Soil forms on the land surface and plays a crucial role in supporting life on Earth. Think of the soil as a blanket covering the Earth's land surface, home to billions of organisms, all part of a symphony orchestra that gives rise to life. These tiny unseen organisms assist in soil formation that allows forests to grow and provide structure and nutrients for shrubs, grasses, wildflowers, fungi, lichens, and moss to grow. The soil is the foundation for life on Earth. It is here that life forms, where flora and fauna thrive, where complex interdependent relationships occur. Soil provides the framework to the mycelium sheath, the network of mycelium that allow for plant communication, nutrient uptake, and ultimately new soil formation.

Permaculturist Aaron Jerad describes bacteria as "the smallest but most abundant member of the soil food web. Often feared but essential, whether directly or indirectly, for the survival of almost all other living organisms on earth."

While there are thousands of different soils in the world, their existence is dwindling due to development, monoculture, erosion, clear-cutting, and fracking, among others. Monoculture is the production of single crops over large amounts of acreage that leads to the increased usage of pesticides and herbicides. Farmers who grow these crops are often subject to signing a contract to purchase genetically modified (GMO) seed and the chemicals that accompany them. This leads to various major problems, including contamination of soil and water, erosion, a decrease in soil life, a decrease in biodiversity on that land, and over time, complete degradation of the once fertile land, the flora, and the fauna. Unfortunately, the damage done by these types of farms has already caused a great deal of irreversible destruction to the environment. Fortunately, there are many large-scale farmers who are transitioning to no-till methods, more humane treatment of animals, pesticide-free growing methods, and smaller-scale operations. Joel Salatin has been planting the way by offering practical advice for farmers who wish to make the transition from conventional farming to no-till farming.

Since the end result of vermicomposting is to have affordable natural fertilizer to give nutrients to your garden, it makes sense to talk about growing food first. The idea of "local foods" began nearly one million years ago with the first hunters and gatherers eating only what they could find in a 100-mile radius. It is only through the globalization of trade and the development of food industry technologies that the concept of local foods was lost to most of us. The modern local foods movement peaked during the victory garden days of World War I and II when canning and preserving fruits and vegetables was the citizen's duty to reduce pressure on the public food supply during wartime. It took a long hiatus postwar through the industrialization of mass food production prompted by the modernization of large-scale farming and the introduction of chemical fertilizers and pesticides and inevitably the growth of grocery store chains in the 1950s. Coincidently, the so-called Green Revolution spawned from the development and production of war chemicals.

While the Green Revolution may have begun as a way to help with starvation, it evolved into something far from it. Wouldn't it have been easier to pass laws making it necessary for people nationwide to have access to a spot for growing their own food? For over five decades, junk food, convenience foods, and prepackaged meals made their way onto kitchen tables around the world, and unfortunately that trend only grows as everyone gets busier. Gardens were replaced with lawns. Real fruit was replaced with artificially flavored vacuum-packed fruit cups swimming in syrup. Home-cooked meals were replaced with Hamburger Helper.

Today, the local foods movement is back. Gardening and self-sufficiency are making a comeback, and we are, in essence, getting back to our roots. While local foods may be slightly more expensive, it helps to think of it in terms of spending a few extra dollars per week to reduce our overall healthcare costs and to improve the well-being of the environment. Local foods grown without pesticides help to improve our health and are a viable form of preventative healthcare. Additionally, purchasing sustainably grown food contributes to the future of the planet. Localize'd food systems significantly reduce the carbon footprint by cutting back on the number of miles that food travels. They also circulate funds back into the local economy. There are plenty of farmers markets around the country that accept SNAP (Supplemental Nutrition Assistance Program) benefits or food stamps, expanding access for low-income families. Locavores on a budget can join CSA (community supported agriculture) farms and supplement with their own backyard garden. The rise of food awareness is paramount for our growth as a healthy, sustainable community. Seeing the world from the potato's-eye view makes us firm believers in the local foods movement as a remedy for the global food crisis.

By teaching and empowering others, especially youth, to grow their own food, we provide them with a sense of purpose, accomplishment, and responsibility. By encouraging them to source food locally, we instill in them a sense of community that fosters respect and commitment and provides a stepping-stone for them to tackle other pressing environmental concerns, such as deforestation, global climate change, air and water quality, natural gas fracking, and exploitative extractive industries.

Good food requires good soil. Good soil requires worms and a variety of other soil-dwelling organisms and microorganisms to sprout life from the soil.

Soil has been labeled as a nonrenewable resource by many scientists, and therefore, measures must be taken to ensure that the soil that is left on Earth will be preserved and held with reverence. In an article in *TIME Magazine* (December 14, 2012), Professor John Crawford of the University of Sydney estimates that in 60 years the topsoil will be depleted:

Some 40% of soil used for agriculture around the world is classed as either degraded or seriously degraded, meaning that 70% of the topsoil, the layer allowing plants to grow, is gone. Because of various farming methods that strip the soil of carbon and make it less robust as well as weaker in nutrients, soil is being lost between 10 and 40 times the rate at which it can be naturally replenished.

Further, he concludes that "microbes need carbon for food, but carbon is being lost from the soil in a number of ways — over-ploughing, the misuse of certain fertilizers, and overgrazing."

If these problems are not immediately addressed, Crawford states there are two major issues of concern. First he predicts the loss of soil productivity will result in a 30% decrease in food production over the next 20 to 50 years. Second, he fears water will reach a crisis point, an issue that is causing conflict all over the world. This is bad news.

The best efforts the human race can make are to:

- Stop relying on big agriculture for our food supply. This means altering our diets to eat with the seasons.
- Support your local farmers: Join a CSA. Shop at the local grocer or farmers markets. Join a co-op or buying club to source local meats, fruits, veggies, eggs, dairy, etc.
- Grow your own fruits, vegetables, and herbs and practice soil-building techniques in the process.
- Leave the soil better than you found it.

- Educate others in your community about the importance of soil building — for the health of the environment, air and water quality, for the health of all life on Earth from the tiny microscopic organisms beneath our feet to insects, reptiles, amphibians, birds, mammals, and humans.
- Become an advocate in your community. Get involved in ways to prevent the depletion of nonrenewable resources.
- Participate in river cleanups and litter cleanups.

For nearly a decade, my husband Eric Stevens and I have been growing food for our community, always using organic methods. For smaller gardens that we have installed, we have used no-till methods. From 2010 to 2016, we co-managed a CSA farm, operating on a shoestring budget that forced us to find creative solutions to issues such as soil fertility, plant health, and increasing crop yields.

We built the vermicompost bins upon our arrival at La Vista. While we did use tillers and tractor implements, we tried to remediate the soil by practicing crop rotation, adding cover crops, compost, straw, leaf mulch, and other organic materials. We used vermicompost (often with worms still in it) to fertilize our crops with living microbes and nutrients, side-dressing each plant in the field with a scoop to give them a jumpstart and facilitate growth and plant vitality.

Fastening three pallets together, we started with a single compost bin under a shade tree. We filled it with straw, fallen leaves, grass clippings, food scraps, shredded cardboard, torn strips of newspaper, as well as small branches and twigs to provide air spaces. We turned the compost a few times and let it sit for a few days. We then purchased a bag of mail-order red wriggler worms from an ad in *Mother Earth News*. After making a little hole in the bin by pushing away some of the compost, we added the worms. Our son got to help, and boy, was that such a neat experience to watch a young little lad holding a hundred worms in his hands. His eyes lit up, and he didn't want to put them in the bin. He wanted to bring them home. But we told him the vital role that worms play and how much they will love their new home, which made it a little easier to say farewell to the worms for now, with the promise that he could visit them each day.

Since my son started at the local Montessori school, I have been teaching gardening lessons there as well as a garden summer camp. The children are so fascinated by the miraculous seed-to-table process, the excitement of planting, harvesting, and saving seed. But nothing seems to strike their interest more than worms and their role in food production and creating soil. Children love gardening and in turn are curious about the food they harvest. Children who garden tend to love vegetables.

Each of us can play a role in building healthy soils. Whether through backyard gardening, composting, vermicomposting, permaculture, adding mycelium to the soil, adding soil amendments, practicing regenerative soil building techniques — every bit helps. On a larger scale, adding cover crops, practicing polyculture and biodynamic farming techniques, and implementing large-scale permaculture methods are good places to start.

After adding the worms seven years ago, we have seen them multiply by the thousands. We have been separating them out and adding them to new piles or giving them away at talks ever since. We have been teaching Vermiculture 101 workshops for several years. We love presenting the Vermiculture 101 workshop as well as the Family Adventures in Vermiculture at the Mother Earth News fairs, across the country; (which happen several times each year). We have no formal degree in the subject matter, so please know that everyone approaches vermicomposting a little bit differently. Our passion for Earth stewardship fuels our drive to want to share the knowledge.

A GOOD GARDEN BEGINS
WITH HEALTHY SOIL

COMPOST:
A GARDENER'S MOST VALUABLE RESOURCE

Avid gardeners are fully aware of the importance of compost. We have seen the enormous difference that it makes on crops such as tomatoes, eggplant, and peppers. We have done experiments planting two rows of identical crops: one row with compost added and one without. The crop with compost doubled in size within just a few short weeks. Most gardeners will talk as long as you let them about their prized compost pile. It is often life-altering when the newbie gardener comes to the exciting realization that over half of their waste can simply be thrown into a bin in a corner of the yard and over time breaks down into the most nutrient rich soil. The concept becomes even more fascinating when observing the similarities between what was happening in my compost bin and what was happening in nature. The typical newbie gardener usually throws all of the veggie ends and recycled brown paper bags in the compost bin and forgets about it for months. When they return, they discover the "black gold."

Ideally, all of our garden beds would be exactly like a compost bin, alive with various layers gently breaking down with no compaction. Building healthy soil is the key to having optimal health in any garden setting. In can be thought of in terms of building the soil's immune system to help fight off unwanted diseases or pests. As non-certified organic CSA farmers, we are often asked questions such as "How do you build healthy soil?" and "What can I add to my soil to make it organic?" Our answer is based on the same concept every time: The soil is a living organism covering the Earth's surface. Like all living things, it needs to be fed proper nutrients to thrive.

It is important to discuss some key elements.

NITROGEN FIXATION AND CARBON SEQUESTERING

Christine Jones, in a *Permaculture News* article (October 2014) stated:

> Nitrogen is a component of protein and DNA and as such, is essential to all living things. Prior to the Industrial Revolution, around 97% of the nitrogen supporting life on earth was fixed biologically. Over the last century, intensification of farming, coupled with a lack of understanding of soil microbial communities, has resulted in reduced biological activity and an increased application of industrially produced forms of nitrogen to agricultural land. Despite its abundance in the atmosphere, nitrogen is frequently the most limiting element for plants. There is a *reason* for this. Carbon, essential to photosynthesis and soil function, occurs as a trace gas, carbon dioxide, currently comprising 0.04% of the atmosphere. The most efficient way to transform carbon dioxide to stable organic soil complexes (containing both C and N) is via the liquid carbon pathway. The requirement for biologically fixed nitrogen drives this process. If plants were able to access nitrogen directly from the atmosphere, their growth would be impeded by the absence of carbon-rich topsoil. We are witnessing an analogous situation in agriculture

today. When inorganic nitrogen is provided, the supply of carbon to associative nitrogen-fixing microbes is inhibited, resulting in carbon-depleted soils. Aggregation is the key. Aggregates are the small "lumps" in soil that provide tilth, porosity and water-holding capacity. Unless soils are actively aggregating, they will not be fixing significant amounts of atmospheric N or sequestering stable forms of carbon. All three functions (aggregation, biological N-fixation and stable C-sequestration) are inter-dependent. The microbes involved in the formation of soil aggregates require an energy source. This energy initially comes from the sun. In the miracle of photosynthesis, green plants transform light energy, water and carbon dioxide into biochemical energy, which is transferred to soil as liquid carbon via an intricate network of mycorrhizal fungi and associated bacteria. Biological nitrogen fixation is the key driver of the nitrogen and carbon cycles in all natural ecosystems, both on land and in water. When managed appropriately, biological nitrogen fixation can also be the major determinant of the productivity of agricultural land. Many farmers around the world are discovering first-hand how the change from bare fallows to biodiverse year-long green, coupled with appropriate livestock management and reduced applications of inorganic nitrogen, can restore natural topsoil fertility. Improving soil function delivers benefits both on-farm and to the wider environment.

The nitrogen cycle is defined by *Encyclopedia Britannica* as the circulation of nitrogen in various forms through nature.

Nitrogen, a component of proteins and nucleic acids, is essential to life on Earth. Although 78 percent by volume of the atmosphere is nitrogen gas, this abundant reservoir exists in a form unusable

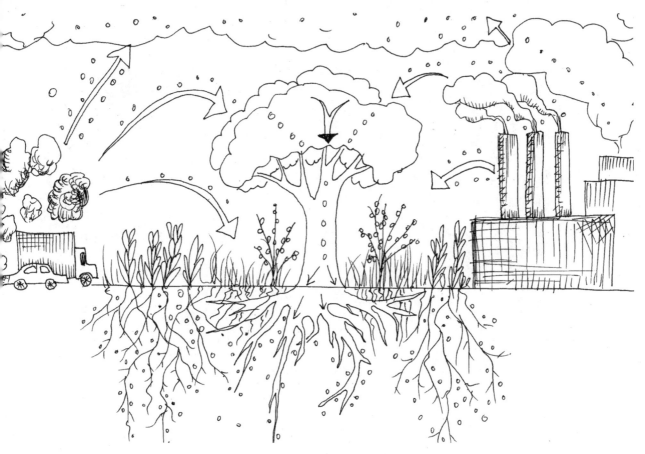

▲ Carbon sequestration. Credit: www.resilience.org/stories/2015-09-02/why-not-start-today-backyard-carbon-sequestration-is-something-nearly-everyone-can-do/

by most organisms. Through a series of microbial transformations, however, nitrogen is made available to plants, which in turn ultimately sustain all animal life. The steps, which are not altogether sequential, fall into the following classifications: nitrogen fixation, nitrogen assimilation, ammonification, nitrification, and denitrification.

Nitrogen fixation, in which nitrogen gas is converted into inorganic nitrogen compounds, is mostly (90 percent) accomplished by certain bacteria and blue-green algae (*see* nitrogen fixation). A

▲ Practicing organic and regenerative farming techniques can help to remedy some of these problems. Planting nitrogen fixing trees, plants and cover crops are a good place to start.

much smaller amount of free nitrogen is fixed by abiotic means (e.g., lightning, ultraviolet radiation, electrical equipment) and by conversion to ammonia through the Haber-Bosch process.

Nitrates and ammonia resulting from nitrogen fixation are assimilated into the specific tissue compounds of algae and higher plants. Animals then ingest these algae and plants, converting them into their own body compounds.

The remains of all living things—and their waste products—are decomposed by microorganisms in the process of ammonification, which yields ammonia. (Under anaerobic, or oxygen-free, conditions foul-smelling putrefactive products may appear, but they too are converted to ammonia in time.) Ammonia can leave the soil or be converted into other nitrogen compounds, depending in part on soil conditions.

Nitrification, a process carried out by nitrifying bacteria, transforms soil ammonia into nitrates, which plants can incorporate into their own tissues.

Nitrates also are metabolized by denitrifying bacteria, which are especially active in water-logged, anaerobic soils. The action of these bacteria tends to deplete soil nitrates, forming free atmospheric nitrogen.

According to Adrian Ayres Fisher, in an *Ecological Gardening* article (September 2015), "carbon sequestration, or pulling carbon out of the air and storing it deep in the ground, as noted environmental journalist Elizabeth Kolbert points out in a recent article, no one knows how to do this."

However, this is not precisely true, though in a modern technological sense of course it is. Anyone who owns or rents a little land on which plants grow can, him or herself, sequester carbon, and may even be doing so at this very moment without even realizing it. It's not hard. Healthy soil does this naturally. All we have to do is help nature along. And as we do so, we can help improve ecosystems, improve soil fertility, and even help endangered species survive. Regenerative farmers and ranchers are doing this in a big way all over the world, though the ones I'm most familiar with are working in the US, in places like North Dakota, Illinois and Minnesota. Even though farming and gardening practice has usually, seemingly inevitably, depleted the soil, scientists such as R. Lal, Christine

▲ It is important to teach future farmers the importance of soil health and land stewardship.

Jones, Michelle Wander, Michel Cavigelli and others, as well as entities such as the Rodale Institute, have shown that regenerative techniques actually rejuvenate the soil and sequester carbon. And, not only is their, and others', long-term research showing how and why this works, but scientists are also teaming up with farmers to demonstrate and study practical techniques—and even conducting classes to teach farmers soil conservation methods. This is vitally important work, since agriculture and other domestic land management is responsible for something like 30% of greenhouse gas emissions worldwide. The key is to help soil store more carbon than is released, while at the same time encouraging nitrogen fixation and general nutrient production. Unfortunately, a number of standard farming and gardening practices prevent these desirable processes.

Here are some actions that each of us can take in our own yards:

- Do not use synthetic fertilizers, pesticides, herbicides, fungicides, insecticides, or other inorganic sprays.
- Reduce the size of your lawn by planting native species and participating in ecological restoration.
- Over-seed lawns with Dutch white clover.
- Don't rake leaves: allow them to decompose, help build soil, and store carbon.
- Use regenerative farming and gardening practices.
- Plant nitrogen-fixing leguminous living mulches between vegetable rows.

COMPOSTING IS AN EXAMPLE OF BIOMIMICRY

The Biomimicry Institute defines *biomimicry* as "an approach to innovation that seeks sustainable solutions to human challenges by emulating nature's time tested patterns and strategies." According to the Regenerative Leadership Institute:

Composting also is an example of biomimicry, which is the process of trying to mimic natural biological systems. Composting speeds the process exhibited in the woods: plant material falls to

> the ground; it weathers and breaks down; and some of it provides benefit for the soil while other components promote the growth of totally different plants.

Good garden soil is essentially a larger version of a compost pile, ideally composed of ongoing layers of the following:

- Small stems and twigs
- Collapsed leaves
- Grass clippings
- Compost
- Worm castings
- Aged sawdust (untreated)
- Living organisms
- Fruit and vegetable scraps
- Other organic matter

Vermiculture is the term given to worm farming, or the use of worms to break down organic material. *Vermicompost,* or worm compost, is a nutrient-rich natural fertilizer. It is similar to compost, but uses worms such as red wigglers and earthworms to help break down organic material. Red wigglers can be purchased at a bait shop, online, or through mail order.

Vermicompost, which is rich in nitrogen, phosphorus, and potassium, also contains macronutrients and micronutrients, which all benefit plant health and stimulate growth. It also adds nutrient-rich minerals back into the soil. Vermicompost can be made into a nutrient-rich tea to water garden plants. We use one part vermicompost to ten parts water. Simply fill a burlap sack, potato sack, or mesh bag with vermicompost. Place the sack in a large bin such as a Rubbermaid container or 55-gallon drum. Fill with water. Steep the bag for a minimum of one day and a maximum of one week.

Worm castings are the final by-product of vermicompost; essentially they are the aggregate, dark brown rich soil medium found at the bottom of the vermicompost bin. They can be added to a seed-starting soil mixture or used to top-dress seedlings in pots and to side-dress larger transplants in a garden bed or field. Worm castings can also be sprinkled on top of small garden beds.

A GOOD GARDEN BEGINS
WITH HEALTHY SOIL

Building healthy soil is the key to having optimal health in any garden setting. Building the soil structure is crucial in the role of fighting off diseases or pests.

While there are thousands of different soils worldwide, their existence is dwindling due to development, monoculture, erosion, the overuse of herbicides and pesticides, and the overall mistreatment of soils. Because soil is a nonrenewable resource, it must be held with reverence. If we don't stand up for it, we will see more and more of the devastating effects of soil degradation in our lifetime.

We need the soil. Soil provides the framework for life on land. It provides structure for forests and a growing medium for food production. Some of the best ways that each of us can contribute to solutions to healthier soil begin with food. Grow your own by practicing backyard permaculture. Localize food systems by supporting area farmers who practice regenerative growing practices. Buy less. Support renewable energy. Plant native flowers, shrubs, and trees. There are so many things we can be doing for the Earth during our short time here to ensure that our children and grandchildren have access to clean air, clean water, and fertile soil to grow their food.

SAMPLE ID	ANALY-SIS DATE	ORGANIC MATTER	CATION EXCHANGE CAPACITY CEC MEQ/100G	PERCENT BASE SATURATION (COMPUTED) % K (+)	% MG (+)	% CA (+)	% H (+)	% NA (+)	SOIL PH	POTAS-SIUM K (+) PPM	MAG-NESIUM MG (+) PPM
1 front	02-16-12	1.6	7.4	3.9	14.5	80.7		0.9	7.2	112	129
Desired Level				3-5	12-16	70-75			6.8	87-144	107-142
1 back	02-16-12	1.7	8.9	5.2	17.0	77.1		0.7	7.4	181	182
Desired Level				3-5	12-16	70-75			6.8	104-174	128-171
GR House	02-16-12	4.3	19.1	5.1	24.7	67.6		2.6	7.4	383	565
Desired Level				3-5	12-16	70-75			6.8	223-372	275-367
SM Garden	02-16-12	2.4	14.7	5.1	18.3	76.0		0.6	7.7	290	322
Desired Level				3-5	12-16	70-75			6.8	172-287	212-282
2 Backleft	02-16-12	1.7	10.2	2.8	17.3	79.1		0.6	7.5	110	212
Desired Level				3-5	12-16	70-75			6.8	119-199	147-196
2 Backright	02-16-12	1.6	8.9	3.5	17.7	78.2		0.6	7.5	122	189
Desired Level				3-5	12-16	70-75			6.8	104-174	128-171
2 Front	02-16-12	1.6	8.7	4.1	16.2	79.1		0.6	7.4	140	169
Desired Level				3-5	12-16	70-75			6.8	102-170	125-167

▲ An example of soil test results.

- Soil-building techniques can be easily implemented in backyard gardens.
- Ditch the pesticides and herbicides.
- Consider backyard chickens or other livestock.
- Each of us can play a role in building healthy soils.

SOIL QUALITY

Quality soil is the most vital aspect of growing organically! A healthy living soil is the key to vibrant and healthy plants. Compost,

| CALCIUM | SODIUM | PHOSPHORUS | | | SULFUR | ZINC | MANGA-NESE | IRON | COPPER | BORON |
| | | | | | | | MICRONUTRIENTS | | | |
CA (+) PPM	NA (+) PPM	P1 (WEAK BRAY 1:7) (-) PPM	P2 (STRONG BRAY 1:7) (-) PPM	BICARB (OLSON) (-) PPM	S (ICAP) (-) PPM	ZN (+) PPM	MN (+) PPM	FE (+) PPM	CU (+) PPM	B (-) PPM
1190	15	30	39	-	8	3.1	15	34	0.8	0.4
1036-1110		25-50	50-100	33	50	5.0	20	20	5.0	2.0
1366	14	42	76	-	9	3.4	14	29	0.9	0.4
1246-1335		25-50	50-100	33	50	5.0	20	20	5.0	2.0
2579	113	159	160	-	170	7.7	11	52	1.4	1.4
2674-2865		25-50	50-100	33	50	5.0	20	20	5.0	2.0
2233	21	109	116	-	9	9.0	7	42	1.3	0.9
		25-50	50-100	33	50	5.0	20	20	5.0	2.0
1621	18	37	56	-	7	4.1	6	31	0.9	0.6
		25-50	50-100	33	50	5.0	20	20	5.0	2.0
1392	12	43	57	-	7	3.4	6	30	0.8	0.5
		25-50	50-100	33	50	5.0	20	20	5.0	2.0
1374	12	49	98	-	6	4.3	7	29	0.9	0.5
		25-50	50-100	33	50	5.0	20	20	5.0	2.0

vermicompost, and other organic soil add nutrients to your soil, improving plant vitality.

All soils are different. A soil analysis or test is a good starting point to determine what nutrients might be lacking and to understand better the composition and personality of your soil. Soil agronomists offer soil analyses. Typically, they collect and analyze samples from multiple quadrants of your field or farm to determine your soil types and which minerals and trace minerals are abundant or lacking. Most soil agronomists also offer custom natural fertilizers that are OMRI (Organic Materials Review Institute) certified, based on test results.

▲ Nature is a good model to follow.

NATURE IS A GOOD MODEL TO FOLLOW

We like to encourage individuals to look at nature, to *really* look.

- Observe the forest floor up close.
- Notice the layers of fallen trees, branches, leaves, twigs, moss, fungi, and other detritus materials all decaying at various rates.
- You will notice the top layer has the appearance of basic mulch.
- Scratch the surface and you will notice the layers below get broken down inch by inch into perfect soil.

- We strive to obtain those rich qualities in the soil by mimicking those natural layers in the substances we add to our own garden soil.

Ideally, all of our garden beds would be exactly like a compost bin, alive with various layers gently breaking down with no compaction. The soil is a living organism covering the Earth's surface. Like all living things, it needs to be fed proper nutrients to thrive.

▲ Layers in the compost pile.

To recap, ideal garden soil is composed of ongoing layers of the following:

- Small stems and twigs
- Fallen leaves
- Grass clippings
- Compost
- Worm castings
- Aged sawdust (untreated)
- Living organisms
- Fruit and vegetable scraps
- Other organic matter

2

THE ESSENTIALITY
OF WORMS

Worms are essential, for the following reasons:

- Often referred to as ecosystem engineers, worms — especially earthworms — play crucial roles in ecosystem functions. Earthworms improve soil structure by opening small channels or pores within the soil structure, which let air and water through, allowing plants to penetrate their roots deeper into the various layers of soil.
- They break down and recycle organic matter into useable growing medium.
- They create space in the soil for bacteria and fungi, which help make nutrients available to plants.
- They increase nutrient availability by adding and incorporating organic matter into the various levels of soil and also by unlocking the nutrients contained within dead and decaying flora and fauna, making nitrogen, phosphorus, trace minerals, and other nutrients available to microorganisms and the roots of plants.
- As part of the food web, they are eaten by predators.

Tunira Bhadauria and Krishan Gopal Saxena concluded:

The soil biota benefits soil productivity and contributes to the sustainable function of all ecosystems. The cycling of nutrients is a critical function that is essential to life on earth. Earthworms (EWs) are a major component of soil fauna communities in most ecosystems and comprise a large proportion of macrofauna biomass. Their activity is beneficial because it can enhance soil nutrient cycling through the rapid incorporation of detritus into mineral soils. In addition to this mixing effect, mucus production associated with water excretion in earthworm guts also enhances the activity of other beneficial soil microorganisms. This is followed by the production of organic matter. So, in the short term, a more significant effect is the concentration of large quantities of nutrients (N, P, K, and Ca) that are easily assimilable by plants in fresh cast depositions. In addition, earthworms seem to accelerate the mineralization as well as the turnover of soil organic matter. Earthworms are known also to increase nitrogen mineralization, through direct and indirect effects on the microbial community. The increased transfer of organic C and N into soil aggregates indicates the potential for earthworms to facilitate soil organic matter stabilization and accumulation in agricultural systems, and that their influence depends greatly on differences in land management practices. (*Applied and Environmental Soil Science,* Vol. 2010, https://www.hindawi.com/journals/aess/2010/816073/)

According to vermiculturists and educators Joel and Kathy Adams:

78% of the Earth's atmosphere is nitrogen. The role of worms in nitrogen fixation is in their symbiotic relationship with the whole soil food web. The bacterial strains that do the heavy lifting of fixation benefit from the worms' cast egestion (poop), mucus production, and decomposition of matter — proving nutrients for nitrifying bacteria and other feeders in the soil food web. The ingestion, digestion, and egestion of organic matter by worms helps break biology down into microbiology, including the important nitrogen fixing bacteria.

During the 19th century, only natural fertilizers were used. Between 1840-1906 Anhydrous ammonia was created and farming was never the same.

▲ Life beneath the soil.

We are growing our food with the same chemicals used to level buildings in the Oklahoma City bombings. With artificial fertilizer, worms get driven out or killed by the toxins. This is a problem for the soil structure as worms serve a significant purpose. In chapter 24 of *Teaming with Microbes*, Jeff Lowenfels and Wayne Lewis make a strong point — no one ever fertilized an old growth forest. There are roughly two million worms per acre in an old growth forest. (Personal communication)

Research scientist Dr. Julia Stevens stated:

Four examples of how microorganisms shape the ecosystems around them, often leading to benefits that can be felt at an observable scale. These examples include:

- The hyphae — branches — of fungi coil through the soil surrounding plant roots; there, predatory fungi await their prey. These fungi release chemicals from lassolike loops to attract unsuspecting nematodes (tiny roundworms) moving through the soil in search of roots to eat. As the nematodes enter these loops, the fungi constrict the lassos, trapping the nematodes to digest them from the inside out. While the fungi have adapted this unique lifestyle as a way to find nutrients, this activity has the added benefit of protecting plant roots from the predation of nematodes.
- Not far from these fungi, other microorganisms are also hard at work making plant food. Nitrogen is the largest component of air and an essential building block of life — yet plants cannot use atmospheric nitrogen. They rely on a group of bacteria that can take this nitrogen gas and transform it into usable nitrogen food. This process is called nitrogen fixation and acts as a natural fertilizer promoting successful plant growth.
- As water infiltrates and moves through soil to the water table below, diverse microorganisms serve as a natural water filter of both chemical and living pollutants. Microorganisms consume the contaminants — thus removing them from the water supplies on which humans depend.
- In a constant competition for space and nutrients, microorganisms in the soil have become especially efficient at fighting and out-competing each other. The importance of these fighting mechanisms was realized when, in the 1920s, Dr. Alexander

Fleming discovered that the common soil fungus Penicillium notatum contaminated and killed his cultures of disease-causing bacteria. Thanks to the follow-up experiments of Dr. Howard Florey, the antibiotic penicillin was isolated and became one of the first commercial antibiotics. Soils remain an important source of new medicines.

These examples exemplify the critical importance of soil microorganisms and our reliance upon them. However, with more microorganisms in a tablespoon of soil than there are people on Earth, there is much to be discovered about what is occurring right beneath our feet. (May 17, 2015, "Inside NC Science: A world of mystery lives underfoot in soils", Newsobserver.com)

SOME WORMS POSE A THREAT

Biologist Andrea Moore stated:

Most earthworms are not native to North America, since the last glacial period stripped the soil of most life: they've been introduced here from Europe. In general, non-native species are a problem worldwide both on land and in the oceans, as some species can become invasive, rapidly changing an ecosystem, and cause negative impacts on other species and humans... New worms pose a major threat to hardwood forests, where they would change the soil structure and growth dynamics of the ecosystem. (fix.com/blog/composting-with-worms, December 12, 2014)

3

ALL ABOUT WORMS

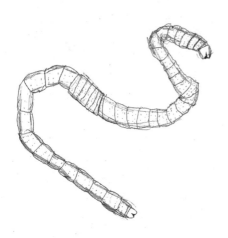

THE ANATOMY
OF A WORM

The anterior of the worm is home to the mouth, which moves decaying matter and microorganisms into the body.

The rings visible on a worm's body are called segments. An adult worm can have over 170 segments. Visible only with a microscope, each segment has small bristles called setae that help the worm to slow down, while the circular and long muscles throughout the worm's body help it to move.

A red wriggler worm has five hearts (technically not actual hearts, rather aortic arches) that contract and release, performing similar functions as the human heart but in a slightly different way. The worm's pseudo hearts essentially squeeze the ventral and dorsal blood vessels, circulating blood through its body.

Worms breathe through their skin and must remain moist in order for oxygen to pass through.

Worms have no eyes. Instead, they have cells near their anterior that are sensitive to light.

The posterior is where worms (via the anus) deposit castings, a fancy word for poop.

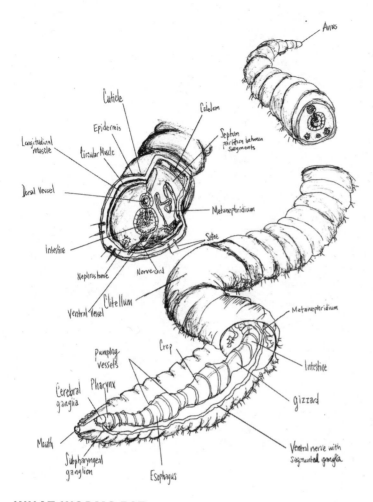

Anus

Cuticle
Epidermis
Longitudinal Muscle
Circular Muscle
Dorsal Vessel
Intestine
Nephrostome
Ventral Vessel
Clitellum

Coelom
Septum partition between Segments
Metanephridium
Setae
Nerve cord

Pumping Vessels
Cerebral ganglia
Pharynx
Crop
Mouth
Subpharyngeal ganglion
Esophagus
Metanephridium
Intestine
gizzard
Ventral nerve with Segmental ganglia

◀ Anatomy of a worm. ADAPTED FROM PEARSON EDUCATION INC, PUBLISHING AS BENJAMIN CUMMINGS

WHAT WORMS EAT

Worms digest microorganisms, protozoa, fungi, bacteria, as well as organic and decaying matter. Their gizzard, near the mouth, breaks down and digests food with help from tiny bits of soil and sand that grind food into smaller particles.

WORM REPRODUCTION

The midsection of a worm, with no segments, is called the clitellum, which forms when a worm is four to six weeks old. It has both female and male reproductive organs (ovaries and testes). Worms join together in opposite directions at the clitellum and exchange mucus.

The sperm is then passed from one worm to the other and stored in sacs. On each worm, a cocoon forms over openings in these sacs, and eggs and sperm are deposited into the cocoon as the worm moves and wiggles out of it. Once released by the worm, the cocoon then closes at both ends for egg fertilization to take place. Cocoons will hatch between two and three weeks and can contain from up to five baby worms measuring under an inch. In six weeks, the cycle continues, and the baby worms will start reproducing. Mary Appelhof concluded that "8 worms can reproduce into 1,500 worms in as little as 6 months; 1,000 worms can reproduce into about 180,000 worms in as little as 6 months under the right conditions."

TYPES OF WORMS

The Oxford Dictionary describes an earthworm as a burrowing segmented worm of the phylum Annelida, which lives in the soil, important in aerating and draining the soil in burying organic matter. Earthworms, ragworms, lungworms, and leeches are all in this large phylum, which are mostly burrowing, aquatic, or free-living, meaning that they are not a part of a parasitic relationship. They generally have a cuticle that covers their typically elongated and segmented body. They possess a locomotory organ (chetae or setae), and respiration occurs through their body surface; excretion occurs through nephridia. They have a blood vascular system and a brain and segmental ganglia associated with their nervous system.

The Natural Resources Conservation Service reported that scientists have identified nearly 7,000 species of earthworms, some as long as 14 inches. The three types are characterized by the depths at which they reside in the soil: epigeic, endogeic, and anecic.

Epigeic earthworms are surface dwellers, residing in areas that are rich in organic matter, feeding on leaf litter, animal feces, and other decaying material. They have dark pigmentation and tend to be present on almost all of the land masses on Earth. *Eisenia fetida*, a variety of epigeic earthworms, are highly adaptable and responsible for renewal of many ecosystems worldwide.

Endogeic earthworms live in the soil and rely on it for food and moisture. They typically stay within a specific soil stratum, tending to burrow horizontally through that specific layer. Their pale skin color typically ranges from pink to grey to even hues of pale blue or green.

Anecic earthworms make somewhat permanent vertical burrows. They actually drag leaf litter and decomposing matter down into them from specific soil layers. These worms typically have darker heads and lighter tails.

▲ Worm with baby.

Charles Darwin studied earthworms for over 40 years. In 1881, he published his research and experiments in *The Formation of Vegetable Mould through the Action of Worms, with Observations on Their Habits*. In his historic work, he studied their eating and burrowing habits, their sensitivity to light and sound vibrations, and their level of intelligence.

After studying Darwin, history scholar, Christopher Lloyd, author of *What on Earth Evolved?*, wrote, "According to Darwin, no living thing has had such a profound impact on history as the earthworm… Wherever earthworms plough, people thrive. When worms perish, societies collapse."

Clive A. Edwards of Ohio State University stated, "Earthworms occur in most temperate soils and many tropical soils. They are divided into 23 families, more than 700 genera, and more than 7,000 species. They range from an inch to two yards in length and are found seasonally at all depths in the soil." (https://extension.illinois.edu/soil/SoilBiology/earthworms.htm)

Worms are divided into several major categories—night crawlers, earth workers, earthworms, composting worms, burrowing worms, surface-dwelling worms — each playing a role in soil, structure, and fertility.

In *Worms Eat My Garbage*, Mary Applehof discussed multiple types of composting worms, with her preference being the red wriggler (*Eisenia fetida*); others were the red tiger (*Eisenia andrei*), the true red worm (*Lumbricus rubellus*), the Indian blue worm (*Perionyx excavatus*), and the African night crawler (*Eudrilus eugeniae*).

She detailed the latter:

Night crawlers play important roles in soil fertility. These large soil dwelling earthworms have extensive burrows extending from the ground surface to several feet deep. They come to the surface on moist spring and fall nights and forage for food, drawing dead leaves, grass, and other organic materials into their burrows where they feed upon it at a later time. Night crawlers perform important soil mixing functions. They take organic material into deeper layers of the soil, mix it with subsoils and that they consume in their burrowing activities and bring mineral subsoils to the surface where they deposit their casts. They also aid in soil aeration and water retention by increasing the rate at which water can penetrate the deeper soil layers.

4

VERMICOMPOSTING BASICS

As discussed in chapter one, vermiculture, or worm farming, is the use of worms to break down organic material. It is a simple way of turning table scraps such as the tops of vegetables, apple cores, banana peels, egg shells, coffee grounds, and even newspaper into vermicompost. The end product is a nutrient-rich natural fertilizer called worm castings. In a vermicompost bin, conditions are maintained for hosting an environment for worm reproduction.

According to Rhonda Sherman of North Carolina State University:

A variety of methods may be used to process large volumes of residuals with earthworms, ranging from land and labor-intensive techniques to fully automated high-tech systems. Types of systems include windrows, beds, bins, and automated raised bioreactors. Choosing which vermicomposting system to use will depend on the amount of feedstock to be processed, funding available, site and space restrictions, climate and weather, state and local regulatory restrictions, facilities and equipment on hand and availability of low cost labor. (http://articles.extension.org/pages/17453/vermicomposting-animal-manure)

BENEFITS OF
BACKYARD VERMICULTURE

Vermiculture can benefit your backyard garden in the following ways:

- It enhances your existing composting operation.
- It introduces composting worms for a high-yield nutrient-rich fertilizer.
- It is similar to compost, but uses worms such as red wigglers and earthworms to help break down organic material.
- It has a higher amount of humus than compost, improving aeration and water retention tremendously.

Vermicompost is rich in nitrogen, phosphorus, and potassium and contains both macronutrients and micronutrients to benefit plant health and stimulate plant growth. It contains worm castings, partially decomposed organic materials, and organic waste with recognizable fragments of plants, food, and detritus materials. When you apply vermicompost, rich minerals are added into the soil. Most vermicompost contains plant growth hormones, increasing plant vitality and yields. In vermicompost, micronutrients that may ordinarily be washed away in heavy rains, such as magnesium and sulfur, are binded.

An article published in 2010 demonstrated that:

Vermicompost contains plant nutrients including N, P, K, Ca, Mg, S, Fe, Mn, Zn, Cu, and B, the uptake of which has a positive effect on plant nutrition, photosynthesis, the chlorophyll content of the leaves and improves the nutrient content of the different plant components (roots shoots and the fruits). The high percentage of humic acids in vermicompost contributes to plant health, as it promotes the synthesis of phenolic compounds such as anthocyanins and fla-vonoids which may improve the plant quality and act as a deterrent to pests and diseases. (*International Journal of the Physical Sciences*, Vol. 5(13), pp. 1964-1973, academicjournals.org/IJPS)

In terms of affordability, vermicomposting is superior. The great product that it yields is by far worth the small investment that it costs to get started. You can actually get started for free if you have a friend who keeps worms already. Just have your system in place first and ask them for about a dozen worms. Within a month or two, your population will start to increase.

In the retail market, natural fertilizers can be very expensive. Finished vermicompost sells for up to $35 for a 20-pound bag. A 20-pound bag of castings can be made in your basement or backyard for pennies, once your initial costs are paid.

If you are using reclaimed materials to build an outdoor bin, you just have to buy the worms and straw bales (to be used as occasional bedding and for insulation during winter months). The costs can really be kept down, as long as you are creative with your building resources.

You could even host a vermiculturist to demonstrate building a worm bin. Any we know would be happy to present a hands-on back-yard workshop. They would probably even bring you starter worms, as long as there were at least five participants and each paid a work-shop fee or gave a small donation for the presenter's time and travel. It would help to have separate piles of reclaimed lumber or pallets, baling wire, and organic materials already prepped, as well as bed-ding (shredded newspaper or office paper).

PURCHASING WORMS

Since there are roughly 1,000 worms per pound, they are counted by weight rather than by count. Worms can typically eat more than their weight per day. For an indoor worm bin, starting with 50 to 100 worms is fine. For an outdoor vermicompost bin, we started with 1,000 worms and they multiplied quickly.

Worms can be mail-ordered. The following are reputable companies that sell red wriggler worms:

- Uncle Jim's Worm Farm: 1-800-373-0555
  www.unclejimswormfarm.com
- Planet Natural: 1-800-289-6656 www.planetnatural.com
- Red Worm Composting: www.redwormcomposting.com
- Gardener's Supply Company: 1-888-833-1412
  www.gardeners.com
- Windy City Worms: wiggle-west@windycityworms.com;
  www.windycityworms.com
- Local Harvest: 1-831-515-5602 www.localharvest.org

Here are some current prices ($US).

- $45 for 2,000 composting worms
- $35.99 for 1,000 Red Composting Worm Mix
- $29.99 for 500 Red Composting Worm Mix
- $29.95 for European Night Crawlers

HOME COMPOSTING

Have a composting system in place. There is an intimidating factor that comes into play with indoor home composting. Beginners often fear the dreadful smell associated with composting. If done right, there is virtually no smell. The following methods have worked best for us after years of kitchen composting:

DO COMPOST

newspaper

Apple core

banana scraps

Veggie scraps

Coffee Grounds

Egg Shell

toilet paper rolls

WORM COMPOSTING

DON'T COMPOST

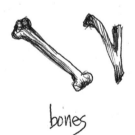

bones

hot peppers

Citrus

garlic

Onions

▲ The do's and don'ts of compost.

- Use a bin with a lid. Cut holes in the lid.
- Add equal parts wet and dry material. Be sure that there is enough oxygen and moisture in the worm bin. Anaerobic composting, the result of too much moisture, gives off a very foul smell. As long as you have bedding and food scraps, as well as enough moisture, you will create the optimal composting environment.
- Keep the bin in an area that is accessible, so that it is not easily forgotten. It should be far enough away from your main living space so that the odor is not detected. We keep ours near the trash can.
- If you are really concerned about the odor and attracting fruit flies, keep the bin right outside your kitchen door or window.

Simple compost bins for kitchen scraps require the following:

- a small trash can with a pedal that lifts the lid
- a five-gallon bucket with a lid
- a small container with a lid (ice cream gallon bucket)

We empty ours every three days, and there is virtually no smell. If you are worried about an odor, keep a can of sawdust nearby and sprinkle on a scoop after each addition to the compost bin.

Several worm bin designs are specifically customized for indoor use. Be sure they have adequate amounts of food and bedding for the worms.

THE DO'S & DON'TS OF COMPOST AND VERMICOMPOST

A compost bin and a vermicompost bin are different. Some items that can go into a compost bin should not go into a vermicompost bin.

Compost Materials

The following items can be composted:

- All food scraps (mainly fruit and vegetable scraps)
- Meat and bones (though it will attract wildlife, sometimes unwanted visitors such as raccoons)
- Dairy (also may attract unwanted visitors)
- Egg shells
- Coffee grounds
- Newspaper (black and white only, no color glossy)
- Cardboard, such as toilet paper and paper towel rolls
- Leaves
- Grass clippings
- Small twigs
- Plants removed from the garden after life cycle is complete. Do not add if they are infested with non-beneficial insects or are diseased.
- Weeds before they go to seed (not invasive weeds)

Vermicompost Materials

The following items can be composted:

- All food scraps
- Egg shells
- Coffee grounds
- Newspaper (black and white only, no color glossy)
- Cardboard, such as toilet paper and paper towel rolls
- Leaves
- Grass clippings
- Small twigs

- Plants removed from the garden after life cycle is complete. Do not add if they are infested with non-beneficial insects or are diseased.
- Weeds before they go to seed (not invasive weeds)

What Not to Compost

It is important not to compost waste that should go to the landfill or be recycled such as plastic, Styrofoam, or any materials that won't decompose. Do not add invasive weeds and diseased or infested plants; instead, burn them away from the garden and compost bin.

PILE DIVISION

On a larger scale, compost can be placed into piles or long rows instead of bins. We like to divide ours into one-year, two-year, and five-year piles. The one-year pile has plenty of worms and microorganisms that are working hard to transform the organic matter into useable growing medium/fertilizer. It contains only materials that will decompose within 12 months, such as food scraps, leaf litter, newspaper, and grass clippings. It has an equal carbon and nitrogen ratio.

The two-year pile contains everything in the one-year pile, but we add cardboard and manures from goats, rabbits, cows, and horses. We also include lots of fallen leaves, straw, and paper goods to this pile and turn it weekly.

The five-year pile contains everything the two-year pile has plus chicken manure. Since this is high in nitrogen, we try to neutralize it by adding more straw.

RESOURCES

Recycled paper and newspaper both make an excellent bedding for worms. Buy a simple paper shredder (after checking that friends and family don't have one that they are not using). Newspaper, thin cardboard, and black and white paper waste can all be shredded and

BEDDING MATERIAL	ABSORBENCY	BULKING POT	C:N RATIO
Horse Manure	Medium-Good	Good	22-52
Peat Moss	Good	Medium	58
Corn Silage	Medium-Good	Medium	38-43
Hay – general	Poor	Medium	15-32
Straw – general	Poor	Medium-Good	48-98
Straw – oat	Poor	Medium	100-150
Straw – wheat	Poor	Medium-Good	127-178
Paper from municipal waste stream	Medium-Good	Medium	170
Newspaper	Good	Medium	116-436
Bark – hardwoods	Poor	Good	131-1285
Bark – softwoods	Poor	Good	563
Corrugated cardboard	Good	Medium	563
Lumber mill waste - chipped	Poor	Good	170
Paper fiber sludge	Medium-Good	Medium	250
Paper mill sludge	Good	Medium	54
Sawdust	Poor-Medium	Poor-Medium	142-750
Shrub trimmings	Poor	Good	53
Hardwood chips, shavings	Poor	Good	451-819
Softwood chips, shavings	Poor	Good	212-1313
Leaves (dry, loose)	Poor-Medium	Poor-Medium	40-80
Corn stalks	Poor	Good	60-73
Corn cobs	Poor-Medium	Good	56-123

▲ Common bedding materials. (Courtesy of Glenn Monroe, Vermiculture Farmers Manual, Organic Agriculture Centre of Canada), https://www.dal.ca/content/dam/dalhousie/pdf/faculty/agriculture/oacc/en/soil/Vermiculture_FarmersManual_gm.pdf

kept in a bin with a tight-fitting lid in the garage or mud room. Ask friends and family to save newspapers for you. You might also check with your local newspaper office to see about getting their leftovers after distribution.

Fall leaves are a great addition to the compost pile and the vermicompost pile/bin. Leaf blowers usually come with an attachment that actually sucks and grinds up leaves and deposits them into a collection bag. This works well because the shredded leaves take less time for the worms to grind up, and they won't compact as much as whole leaves in the compost bin.

Grass clippings from untreated lawns are a wonderful addition to the compost pile and the vermicompost pile/bin. Lawn mowers may have a catchment container or bag for collecting clippings, which can then be added with leaf litter to the bins. This should only be done when a lawn is not treated with chemical pesticides.

Sawdust from untreated lumber can be added to a vermicompost bin. If you have a ton of sawdust from treated lumber, you may be able to age it first by combining it in a separate pile with manure. Lumber mills could be a great resource for untreated sawdust.

Wood chips make an excellent filler material for long-term composting and are especially helpful for adding a carbon component to your large pile, for aging manure, and for a base layer in a long windrow system.

Spent grains are an excellent by-product from the brewing process. Readily available year round from most large breweries, they can be a good source of food for microorganisms in the vermicompost bin during winter when vegetable scraps are not readily available. There are mixed reviews on using them for vermicomposting because of the amount of heat they let off when decomposing, as well as how they change the pH of the pile. Using spent brewing grains in the compost pile first would be a good idea. Let them start decomposing and cool down a bit. Do not put fresh spent grains directly into the compost pile; rather, age them for one to two weeks. One method for aging is to use a five-gallon bucket with several holes drilled in the bottom for drainage and airflow. Place about four handfuls of chip mulch at the bottom, add spent grains, and top with several more handfuls of chip mulch. This will allow the spent grains to cool off a bit, and decomposing will start after one to two weeks. Be sure to only add a few handfuls at a time in one corner of the bin. Do not cover the bin with spent grains, because you want the worms to be able to retreat if an area of the bin gets too warm for them.

Coffee grounds are readily available from most coffee shops. If they don't separate their grounds from the garbage, you could offer to provide a few clean buckets for them to dispense the grounds into. You can schedule a weekly pickup and drop off clean buckets each time. This is a great resource, especially if you are doing a large vermicompost system or windrow.

Animal manure is a great addition to the compost pile. Pre-composted or aged manure is better for the vermicompost bin. Some animal manures are better than others. Most offer good nutrition for worms, such as cattle, poultry, sheep, goat, hog, rabbit, and horse manure. Weed seeds in animal manure are often a disadvantage, but pre-composted manure can still be used. In most cases, the seeds need to reach a certain temperature in order to become non-viable. This factor varies for different types of manure and weeds.

NO- TO LOW-BUDGET GARDENING
The following materials and supplies are very useful to the backyard gardener. Some of these can be found in your household, while others can be sourced free or at low cost in your own community.

▶ Glenn Monroe, Vermiculture Farmers Manual, Organic Agriculture Centre of Canada, https://www.dal.ca/content/dam/dalhousie/pdf/faculty/agriculture/oacc/en/soil/Vermiculture_FarmersManual_gm.pdf

- Compost: Most city parks have a free composting system. Usually, you need to haul it yourself in a pickup truck.
- Burlap sacks: Most coffee roasters will give burlap sacks for free, especially to community gardens.
- Wood chips: Tree-trimming companies will often deliver wood chips to community gardens for free. If you see a tree trimmer in

FOOD	ADVANTAGES	DISADVANTAGES	NOTES
Pre-composted food wastes	Good nutrition; partial decomposition makes digestion by worms easier and faster; can include meat and other greasy wastes; less tendency to overheat	Nutrition less than with fresh food waste (Frederickson et al, 1997)	Vermicomposting can speed the curing process for conventional composting operations while increasing value of end product (Georg 2004; Fredrickson, op. cit.)
Biosolids (human waste)	Excellent nutrition and excellent product; can be activated sludge, septic sludge; possibility of waste management revenues	Heavy metal and/or chemical contamination (from municipal sources); odor during application to beds (worms control fairly quickly); possibly of pathogen survival if process not complete	Vermitech Pty Ltd. In Australia has been very successful with this process, but they use automated systems; EPA-funded tests in Florida demonstrated that worms destroy human pathogens as well as does thermophilic composting (Eastman et al., 2000)
Seaweed	Good nutrition; results in excellent product, high in micronutrients and beneficial microbes	Salt must be rinsed off, as it is detrimental to worms; availability varies by region	Beef farmer in Antigonish, NS, producing certified organic vermicompost from cattle manure, bark, and seaweed
Legume hays	Higher N content makes these good feed well as reasonable bedding	Moisture levels not as high as other feeds, requires more input and monitoring	Probably best to mix this feed with others, such as manures
Grains (e.g. feed mixtures for animals, such as chicken mash)	Excellent, balanced nutrition, easy to handle, no odor, can use organic grains for certified organic product	Higher value than most feeds, therefore expensive to use; low moisture content; some larger seeds hard to digest and slow to break down	Danger: Worms consume grains but cannot digest larger, tougher kernels; these are passed in castings and build up in bedding, resulting in sudden overheating (Gaddie, op cit)
Corrugated cardboard (including waxed)	Excellent nutrition (due to high-protein glue used to hold layers together); worms like this material; possible revenue source from WM fees	Must be shredded (waxed variety) and/or soaked (non-waxed) prior to feeding	Some worm growers claim that corrugated cardboard stimulates worm reproduction
Fish, poultry, offal; blood, wastes; animal mortalities	High N content provides good nutrition, opportunity to turn problematic wastes into high-quality product	Must be pre-composted until past thermophilic stage	Composting of offal, blood wastes, etc. is difficult and produces strong odors. Should only be done with in-vessel systems; much bulking required.

FOOD	ADVANTAGES	DISADVANTAGES	NOTES
Cattle manure	Good nutrition; natural food, therefore little adaptation required	Weed seeds make pre-composting necessary	All manures are partially decomposed and thus ready for consumption by worms
Poultry manure	High N content results in good nutrition and a high-value product	High protein levels can be dangerous to worms, so must be used in small quantities; major adaptation required for worms not used to this feedstock. May be pre-composted but not necessary if used cautiously (see Notes)	Some books (e.g., Gaddie & Douglas 1975) suggest that poultry manure is not suitable for worms because it is so "hot"; however research in Nova Scotia (GEORG, 2004) has shown that worms can adapt if initial proportion of PM to bedding is 10% by volume or less
Sheep/Goat manure	Good nutrition	Require pre-composting (weed seeds); small particle size lead to packing, necessitating extra bulking material	With the right additives to increase C:N ratio, these manures are also good beddings
Hog manure	Good nutrition; produces excellent vermicompost	Usually in liquid form, therefore must be dewatered or used with large quantities of highly absorbent bedding	Scientists at Ohio State University found that vermicompost made with hog manure outperformed all other vermicomposts, as well as commercial fertilizer
Rabbit manure	N content second only to poultry manure, therefore good nutrition; contains very good mix of vitamins & minerals; ideal earth-worm feed (Gaddie, 1975)	Must be leached prior to use because of high urine content; can overheat if quantities too large; availability usually not good	Many U.S. rabbit growers place earthworm beds under their rabbit hutches to catch the pellets as they drop through the wore mesh cage floors
Fresh food scraps (e.g., peels, other food prep waste, leftovers, commercial food processing wastes)	Excellent nutrition, good moisture content, possibly of revenues from waste tipping fees	Extremely variable (depending on source); high N can result in overheating; meat & high-fat wastes can create anaerobic conditions and odors, attract pests, so should NOT be included without pre-composting	Some food wastes are much better than others: coffee grounds are excellent, as they are high in, not greasy or smelly, and are attractive to worms; alternatively, root vegetables (e.g., potato culls) resist degradation and require a long time to be consumed

your neighborhood, ask them to deliver to your yard. Put down a few tarps to prevent a large mess and for easy hauling once the pile gets low.

- Crates: Some bakeries and restaurants will give away old crates.
- Pallets: Some large businesses such as grocery stores, nurseries, and hardware stores will give away pallets to community gardens or backyard gardens. It is best to get pallets that are labeled HT (heat treated).
- Straw bales: Straw bales make excellent additions to the backyard garden. Several bales can be formed into a rectangle and used as garden beds, compost piles, worm habitats, etc.

For seed starting, these items can be diverted from the landfill and reused:

- Toilet paper rolls
- Paper towel rolls, cut into sections
- Newspapers, folded into cubes
- Cardboard boxes
- Coffee bags
- Recycled soda or water bottles with the tops cut off

GARDENING TIPS: WATER CONSERVATION

Rainwater catchment is a simple and effective way to conserve water, which can then be run through drip irrigation lines to water garden beds.

Dig small narrow trenches or swales around raised garden berms to retain water.

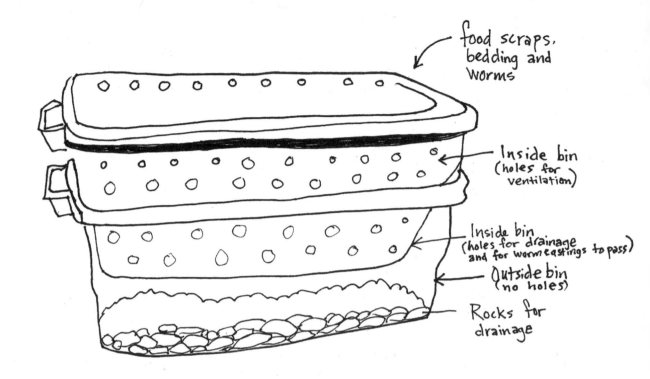

food scraps, bedding and worms

Inside bin (holes for ventilation)

Inside bin (holes for drainage and for worm castings to pass)

Outside bin (no holes)

Rocks for drainage

▲ Standard indoor worm bin made with two Rubbermaid containers.

As you are planting, add water into a trench first if you are planting into a row, or add to each hole before you transplant. This gives the plants enough water for a few days or even a week.

When watering a small garden, water the base of each plant instead of the whole bed. This helps to conserve water.

STANDARD WORM BIN

A typical worm bin is made with two Rubbermaid containers, one with several holes drilled on all four sides and three dozen holes drilled through the bottom. The second container, which will act as a catchment for any liquid, should also have several dozen holes drilled through all four sides, but none on the bottom.

The bottom of the worm bin should have a layer of small pebbles, river rocks, or sand. This will prevent water buildup and promote drainage.

Add the worm bedding — a mixture of shredded paper or torn newspaper, leaf litter, grass clippings, and small pieces of cardboard, such as toilet paper rolls — and spray with water until the mixture is wet.

The bedding should sit until it reaches the correct temperature. It should stay below 90°F (32°C) for at least two days. Once the optimum temperature has been reached, push aside the bedding, add the worms, and cover with the bedding. Food scraps can then be added slowly. A rule of thumb among well-known vermiculturists is that worms can eat their weight in one day. For example, one pound of worms will go through one pound of food scraps daily.

After one to two months, harvest the bottom layer of vermicompost. Add a few handfuls of new worm bedding. Continue adding kitchen scraps, and the cycle will continue. (Adapted from Goorganicgardening.com)

For an educational worm bin in a classroom setting, you can find many designs for sale through websites that specialize in science curriculum. To make your own, you will need the following materials:

- 2 sheets of clear plexiglass (each cut to 18" × 24")
- A box of weatherproof screws (1¼ inch)
- A small plastic container, shoe box size (collects excess liquid, making instant worm tea)
- An 8-foot piece of wood, 1 inch thick × 10 inches wide (untreated pine is ideal)

Cut three 24-inch pieces, for the two sides and lid. Cut one 22½" piece for the bottom.

You should be left with a little strip of wood about 1½ by 10 inches. Cut into three pieces to be used as handles to transport the worm bin between classrooms. First cut 4" for the lid handle, then cut the remaining piece, in half to give you two 3" handles for the sides.

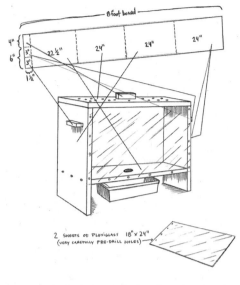

8 foot board

4"
6"
22 ½"
24"
24"
24"
3"
½"

2 SHEETS OF PLEXIGLASS 18" x 24"
(VERY CAREFULLY PRE-DRILL HOLES)

▲ A sample design of an educational worm bin with a viewing window.

▶ A finished example of an educational worm bin with a viewing window.

Lay out all of your pieces in an organized manner so that you don't lose track of which piece is which.

Before assembling, I highly advise you predrill holes for the screws to prevent splitting the wood. When predrilling the plexiglass, be extra cautious not to crack it. This can be achieved by drilling slowly and with very little pressure (the pressure is what will cause it to crack).

Use the diagram to the left as a guide. With a pencil, mark all of the areas to drill. Drill all of the holes and screw the corresponding wood pieces together first (except for the lid). Next, fasten the plexiglass windows to the wood structure. Important: When screwing down the plexiglass, take extra caution to drill very slowly and back off when you begin to contact the plexiglass, as it will crack very easily. A recommended option would be to get rubber washers for the screws to further avoid cracking.

5

COMPOST AND VERMICOMPOST DESIGNS FOR YOUR BACKYARD

This chapter covers some basic designs for building compost or vermicompost bins in your own backyard and includes detailed instructions for using reclaimed/repurposed materials.

SIMPLE COMPOST BOXES

Simple elevated worm boxes can be built using untreated wood and chicken wire or galvanized hardware cloth as a base. Place catchment bins underneath for easy worm harvesting.

Wire Fence Cylinder Compost Bin

Use a panel of scrap wire fencing, roughly ten feet long, with holes no smaller than 2" × 4". To form a cylinder, fasten the ends together with baling wire (overlapping them a few inches for extra support) or zip ties.

This design is great because over time you can actually create raised beds in predetermined areas where you have placed one or more wire cylinder. You can use just one, or create multiples to place in predetermined areas you would like to have raised beds. With the wire cylinder, it is best to start the bins in the summer for a ready-to-go raised bed the following spring. Fill compost to the brim (leaf mulch, grass clippings, food scraps, and straw). There is no need to

▲ Wire fence cylinder compost bin.

turn this bin; just keep adding organic material, and after six to eight months, simply lift the wire cylinder and you have a ready-to-plant garden bed in the spring.

Basic Cube Compost Bin

A simple compost bin can be made using reclaimed pallets, preferably heat-treated ones marked with the letters HT. Securely fasten four pallets together upright with baling wire. Organic materials are added that are broken down by living organisms, microbes, fungi, and bacteria.

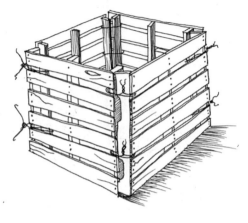

▲ Basic cube compost bin.

Vermicompost bin

A vermicompost bin is essentially the same as a compost bin except that worms are added to help break down materials quicker. Worm castings can be harvested and used as organic fertilizer after about four months. A vermicompost bin can also be built using reclaimed heat-treated pallets. Construct it in the same way except, add a built-in trapdoor or removable slats to harvest worm castings.

For each design, place the fastened bin in a permanent area of your yard with one open end directly on the soil. It is not necessary to remove the grass in this location. To best activate the composting process, fill the bin with leaves, grass clippings, straw, and other organic matter. You may then begin adding kitchen scraps such as fruit and vegetable ends and peels, egg shells, and coffee grounds. Avoid adding meat, dairy, oils, and citrus fruits.

Turn your compost regularly with a pitchfork to speed up the process, turning occasionally in a vermicompost bin to help aerate the compost. Do not cover the compost bin. It should be open to the elements. During dry spells, you may need to add water to your compost bin. Vermicompost bins can be built in boxes under a shelter for worm casting collection. If you want to build healthy soil and attract beneficial microbes, it is best to have the bin open to the elements and open to the soil below, rather than a closed container.

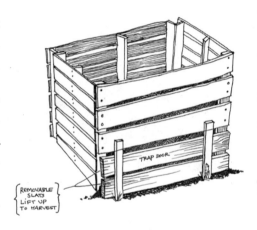

▲ Vermicompost bin.

PERMACULTURE WORM BIN DESIGN

Worm Bin Grow Box

Build a standard worm box with a hard plastic mesh front (with holes large enough for the worms to freely move back and forth). Build an additional box onto the front of the bin, where the mesh is, and plant your favorite garden varieties there.

Ann and Gord Baird's Veggie Washing Station/Worm Bin/Worm Tea Collector

Ann and Gord Baird, permaculturists with Eco-Sense, believe in stacking functions and keeping designs simple. They designed a simple way to conserve and utilize water by building a worm composter right next to a vegetable washing station. The washing station sink drains into a five-gallon bucket; this empties into a worm bin with holes at the bottom, resting in a water drum with a spout, which is raised off the ground. A separate bucket collects the worm tea below. When washing veggies, they pour the wash water into the worm bin, and it flows through to the collection drum. This process saves water, gives nutrients from food waste to worms, and uses worm tea to water their fruit and vegetable plants.

Bath Tub Worm Farm

Repurposing items that would ordinarily go into a landfill is necessary for those on a budget and a practical way to intercept landfill waste. For example, an old claw-foot tub with a few unrepairable holes makes the perfect worm bin. Build a frame out of reclaimed materials or just rest the tub on stacks of cinder blocks. A separate container resting underneath can be easily removed when worm tea is ready to be harvested.

Patio Bench Worm Bin

This design is adapted from *Worms Eat My Garbage* by Mary Appelhof from Seattle Tilth. Build a worm box using a 4-foot-by-8-foot sheet of ½-inch exterior plywood and five or six pieces of framing lumber (construction grade 2" × 4"). Cut the plywood into the sizes shown to the right. Attach to a lumber frame. It can be weatherproofed with outdoor non-toxic stain or varnish.

Midwest Permaculture's Worm Tower

This design is specific to individual garden beds. A large pipe with several dozen holes drilled through it is inserted into the ground. It provides a habitat for worms that have underground access to the soil in the bed. The concept behind this design is that the worms have plenty of access to nutrition and moisture and are able to explore their preferred habitat within the beds. They aerate the soil by adding air pockets that permit roots to go deeper and distribute castings at various levels, offering plenty of nutrition to the plants. This wonderful design removes a lot of the grunt work for the gardener.

One simple design uses two five-gallon buckets. Cut off the bottom and the top of one bucket and drill holes all over the other one (50 or more evenly spaced holes). Fit the first bucket inside the second. In a garden bed, dig a hole the size of one bucket. Insert the bucket and add a little soil around it. Next, add the ingredients for the worm farm. Fill the bucket 1/3 full with soil, add equal parts manure, veggie scraps, water, and a burlap sack, and cover with a lid. Evenly distribute a pound of worms around the outside of the bucket. Cover with the remaining soil. Add veggie scraps each week and be sure the worm farm is kept moist. (Based on design by Inga van Dyk.)

Bill and Becky Wilson have a very simple design for a worm tower, using three simple steps:

1. Drill ¼" holes into a PVC or plastic tube so that the worms can move freely in and out. The tube should be between 2 feet and

Visit midwestpermaculture.com for more great garden ideas.

Rabbit Cage over Worm Bins

Another example of stacking functions is keeping rabbits above open worm bins. The concept is that the rabbit droppings fall through holes in the cages into the bins, keeping the cages clean and providing an ongoing supply of manure for the worm bins. The rabbit cage is built with scrap lumber and chicken wire or hardware cloth. The holes should be large enough for the droppings to fall through but small enough so that the rabbits' paws do not get trapped.

Straw Bale Worm Bin

A simple worm bed can be made using six straw bales (2 long by 1 wide) to form a rectangle in an area of your yard that gets partial shade, such as under a tree. Fill with leaves, newspaper, grass clippings, food scraps, and non-diseased plant remnants from the garden.

Cinder Block Worm Bin

For those who sell worms as a business, Sierra Worm Solutions makes worm beds using cinder blocks that provide insulation during the winter and keep worms confined. The beds are three cinder blocks wide, two tall, and five long. Fill with leaves, newspaper, grass clippings, food scraps, and non-diseased plant remnants.

Woven Willow Worm Bins

If you are unable to buy lumber or have no access to scrap lumber or power tools, you can construct a worm bin using willow branches, young bamboo, or other long pliable branches (as well as some thicker branches), a hand saw, hammer, and nails. From this design you can make permanent or moveable beds. Strip the leaves from eight branches (at least three inches in diameter) that are flat at one end and pointed at the other. Using a hammer or sledge hammer, tap them into the ground in a square with four pieces at each corner and four in between. Holes may need to be slightly predug. Then weave the willow branches or bamboo between the branches and fasten with nails at the corner posts. For a moveable bed, make four separate windows using two long branches for the top and bottom, two smaller ones for the sides, and three smaller ones fastened evenly between the two end posts. Weave the willow or bamboo between the vertical branches.

▲ Woven branches make a beautiful compost or vermicompost bin.

Large Branch Bin

A large branch bin can be made from a fallen tree limb. Use long weatherproof nails or screws to fashion branches in a square or rectangle using the log stacking method. Fill with leaves, newspaper, grass clippings, food scraps, and non-diseased plant remnants.

Worm Hive

The worm hive is a multilayered, stackable worm composting bin system designed by Crystal Henson (momisanunderstatement.blogspot.com).

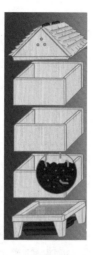

Each layer consists of four solid wood sides with an open top and a bottom covered in 1/4 inch hardware screen. They are designed to stack and interlock. The top layer is covered with a simple hinged wood lid with a few air holes for ventilation. The open bottom and air holes in the lid help maintain air flow to reduce odor and increase oxygen to worms and beneficial bacteria. The bottom layer is filled with some worms, bedding and food scraps then topped with shredded paper. Continue feeding in this layer until full, then place new bedding and food scraps in the next layer up. The worms will naturally migrate up towards the food through the mesh, leaving harvestable castings. The bottom layer rests in a four-legged frame which has a fine aluminum mesh on its bottom and suspends the stack overtop of a plastic catch-bin. Any excess moisture will pass through the boxes to the bin at the bottom, where it can be removed and the compost tea fed to plants. As the worms migrate upwards, the lower level is removed and the castings sifted by shaking the layer, allowing them to pass through the screen. After the layer is emptied, any worms and unprocessed biomass can then be returned to the full layer and the empty one now becomes the top.

The dimensions for the worm hive are 15" wide by 10" deep by 22" high. For more designs and gardening tips, visit Crystal's blog at momisanunderstatement.blogspot.com.

Stacked Crate Bin with Water Spout

Stacked milk crates or rectangular crates can be used like the worm boxes in the worm hive design. A water spout can be added to the bottom bin, and the crates can be elevated to allow worm tea to be harvested.

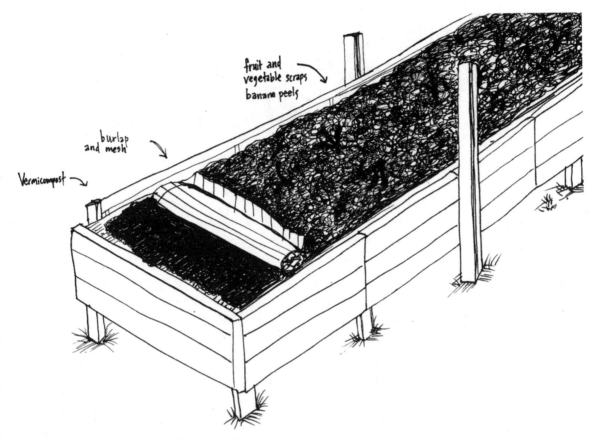

fruit and
vegetable scraps
banana peels

burlap
and mesh

Vermicompost

▲ Elevated worm bins inspired by Growing Power.

LARGER VERMICOMPOST OPERATIONS

Growing Power, founded by Will Allen, manages a large-scale vermicompost operation in Milwaukee, Wisconsin. It holds about 5,000 pounds of compost in raised beds down the center of a high tunnel. They break the compost down (it takes about six to eight months), pre-sift it, and then bring it into the worm bins. They layer about 5,000 pounds of worms in between the layers of soil. For approximately four months, the worms break down the organic material into a usable form. This increases beneficial bacteria by 14 times, so the end result is nutrient rich.

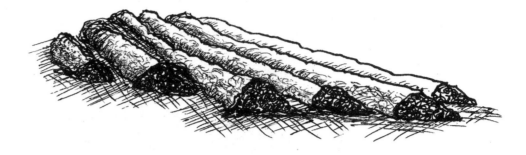

▲ An example of a windrow system.

Once the worm castings are ready to harvest, they place a 16-mesh screen over the worm bin. They then add compost on top of it so that the worms go through the screen to the top where the compost is. The screens are temporarily lifted off the bins and set aside, and they harvest the castings using five-gallon buckets. New compost is added to the worm bins, and the worms and food scraps are returned to the bins as well.

Check Growing Power's impressive worm farming operation at growingpower.org.

WINDROWS

Windrows vary by size and scale. However, their basic concept is a long and often narrow berm of organic decaying material. For example, food waste, particularly fruits and vegetables, can be diverted from the landfill and placed in long narrow piles with chip-mulched pathways. Carbon materials such as leaves or old newspapers can be added to the berms. Worms can be placed evenly over the windrows, and they will immediately get to work.

STOCK TANKS

Kathy and Joel Adams house their worms in elevated stock tanks with spigots. They have had a great deal of success keeping the moisture level of the worm bins between 70% and 85%. Kathy believes that the worms will die in a moisture level below 50%. They also keep a worm pile in wood chips. They add food scraps and peat moss and monitor the pH level regularly. They water their bins regularly but cover them if rain is forecast. They do not use tap water in their worm bins. According to them, "one worm can produce approximately 600 offspring in one year."

6

CARING FOR YOUR VERMICOMPOST BIN

▲ Show your worms some love.

The vermicompost bin should have a sweet earthy smell. It should not give off an offensive odor. If it does begin to smell bad, that may be a sign of an anaerobic environment. In this case, try turning it and add more carbon material, such as straw, wood chips, paper bedding, or cardboard throughout the entire bin. If slime has developed, your bin may be too far gone. If so, you can transfer that to an outdoor compost pile and combine it with wood chips, paper towel rolls, newspapers, etc.

FEEDING YOUR WORMS

As mentioned in chapter 4, worms eat more than their weight each day. As a general rule, one pound of worms needs at least one pound of food source daily. Proper nutrition is key to maintaining your worm bin.

Green Leaf Worm Farm recommends using a base of 18 inches of peat moss, corrugated cardboard, and shredded paper. Corrugated cardboard provides good habitat for raising worms. Because they believe worms need diversity in their diet to produce higher-quality nutrient-rich vermicompost, they feed their worms the following items.

Worm Chow

Buy worm chow or make your own using the following recipe:

12 egg shells (boil for a few minutes first)

Coffee grounds

1 cup oats

1 cup cornmeal

1 cup buckwheat

1 cup wheat berries

¼ tsp sugar

Boil egg shells for a few minutes. Drain and blend in a food processor. Add remaining ingredients and grind thoroughly.

Additional Worm Food

Unrefined masa flour and whole wheat flour in small amounts

Azomite®: 100% natural, organic, and unrefined substance that contains over 100 trace elements

Volcanic sand: helps worms to process and grind down organic materials

Coffee grounds and filters: help to stimulate the worms to eat and reproduce

Organic mineral block: has plenty of vitamins for the worms

Cold manure: use goat or rabbit manure to feed worms

Feeding schedules depend on the amount of worms in your operation.

Additional Worm Food/Grit Options

- Ground oyster shells
- Rock dust
- Stale grains, pasta, cereal, etc.
- Juice pulp (leftover from juicing)
- Stale bread

(Please note: this worm food combination is for a large-scale worm farming operation. Scale down or omit certain ingredients as you see fit.)

Additional Worm Food Recipe

5 cups chicken layer feed

2 cups rice bran (source of carbon, vitamins, and trace elements)

2 cups alfalfa pellets (good source of protein, trace elements, calcium, and B, C, E, and K vitamins)

1 cup lime (agricultural grade)

1 cup whole wheat flour (good source of protein, trace elements, calcium, and B, C, E, and K vitamins)

1 cup powdered milk (good source of protein, trace elements, calcium, and B, C, E, and K vitamins)

Mix ingredients thoroughly in a five-gallon bucket, secure the lid, and store in a cool, dark area.

VERMICOMPOST BIN CONDITIONS

Temperature Regulation

Optimal temperature for a worm bin varies by climate, elevation, time of year, and location indoors or outdoors bin. A general rule is to keep the minimum temperature at 50°F to 80°F (10°C–26°C). The worms may survive extreme temperatures if they have the right moisture content and shade or insulation. Some vermiculturists have overwintered outdoor worms in below-freezing temperatures. Others don't like to stress their worms or risk losing them and will bring their worms inside their garage for the winter.

Moisture Content

Since worms breathe through their skin, their habitat should remain moist but not too moist. The proper balance of moisture and air flow is important. Standing water should never be present in a worm bin. It should also never dry out completely.

Proper Drainage

There should always be a drainage system in place for indoor worm bins. Holes drilled into the bin will usually suffice. More complicated worm bin designs have mesh screens to allow drainage but prevent flies and other insects from entering the bins.

Ventilation/Air Flow

Since worms produce carbon dioxide, air flow is important. Having plenty of bedding in place ahead of time will help create air pockets. Other ideas are to add toilet paper polls throughout the bin facing in different directions.

Insulation during
the Winter Months

Several methods can be used to insulate the worms during the winter months. Our favorite is to simply cover the worms with tons of leaves. We go on secret twilight missions driving around neighborhoods that we know use sustainable landscaping methods. We collect the brown leaf litter bags near the trash cans that people set out who don't want leaves in their yards. Also, before the temperatures get below freezing, we stack straw bales all around the bins to insulate them. Unless heavy snowfall is predicted, we rarely cover our bins. Then we just cover them with sheets of plywood.

The following list has ideas from friends and fellow worm farmers who have had luck overwintering their worms:

- Use a compost bin with a lid and just fill it with lots of organic material. Add a few layers at the top of the bin and close lid for the winter.
- Cover bin with burlap sacks.
- Cover bin with old tin scraps.
- Cover pile with an old blanket.
- Cover pile with an old door.
- Cover pile with a tarp and a few sandbags.

HARVESTING WORM CASTINGS, MAKING WORM TEA, AND GARDEN APPLICATIONS

This chapter discusses how to harvest, sift, and store the worm castings, as well as how to collect the liquid that drains from the bin and store it.

SIMPLE METHODS FOR HARVESTING WORM CASTINGS

Because worm castings are essentially worm waste (manure), the harvesting process is different for each bin design, with the common goal being the removal of the bottom few inches that are fully decomposed.

There are several methods for harvesting worm castings, from a simple screen to a more complex casting tumbler. You can customize them based on your budget, the size of your operation, and your carpentry skills.

Small Worm Bins

For small indoor worm bins, place watermelon rinds or banana peels into the worm bin the night before you wish to harvest the castings. This gives the worms a reason to come to the surface, usually congregating on the peels and rinds. Simply put the peels, rinds, and worms in a separate container while you sift and harvest the rest of the worm castings.

Dump out the contents of your worm bin onto a large tarp. Hand sort all of the worms you see into the separate bin (with the majority of the worms, banana peels, and rinds). Pick out any large clumps of material that has not broken down yet and return them to the worm bin.

Here are two methods from Mary Appelhof's *Worms Eat My Garbage*:

▲ Sifter box used over a wheelbarrow.

Dump and hand sort by making cone shaped piles, adding bright light to prompt worms to go to the bottom of the piles and then to remove the piles of worm castings and add them to a separate bucket. The worms can then be collected and weighed and added back to the worm bin with new bedding and food scraps.

Let the worms do the sorting by pulling all of the vermicompost to one side of the worm bin, add new bedding to the vacant side and bury food scraps in new bedding. The worms will move into the new bedding in search of food. The vermicompost can be removed after 2-3 months and replaced with new food and the process can continue.

A kitchen colander or mesh strainer could work for separating castings. The screen must have holes large enough for the castings to go through, leaving the worms and organic material that has not yet been broken down on the top of the screen.

Sifter Box

You can make a simple sifter box any size you wish, but 2' by 2' or 2½' by 2½' work well to fit over a standard wheelbarrow. Simply screw together untreated scrap lumber to make a frame. Cut galvanized mesh screen to fit the window and fasten using screws.

To sift, place a few handfuls of vermicompost in the sifter box. Shake them back and forth multiple times over the wheelbarrow.

▲ Example of rotary sifter.

The worm castings should fall through the screen and into the wheelbarrow. The remnants on top of the screen, such as small pieces of mulch and twigs and larger food scraps, can be added back to the vermicompost bin.

Galvanized Hardware Cloth

Will Allen has multiple worm boxes that are fairly shallow but wide. When the castings are ready to be harvested, he places galvanized hardware cloth or screen over them and places food scraps such as banana peels and watermelon rinds on the top. The worms come up to the surface, through the hardware cloth, to eat the decaying matter. He lifts off the screen, adds the worms and scraps on it to a new unfinished worm bin, and then harvests the finished bin.

Larger Operations

A large rotary sifter, or a trommel, can be made using scrap materials such as bicycle rims, lumber, zip ties, five-gallon buckets, metal pipes, and PVC pipes. See illustration to the left.

Further, these contraptions can be made in a way that they can be bicycle powered.

Storing Castings

Castings can be stored in five-gallon buckets in a clean, cool, and dark environment. The experts at Sierra Worm Composting recommend the following:

The cardinal rule in castings is that you don't want them to dry out. Keeping them at 20% moisture ensures microbial life. Microbes die if the castings dry out completely. Depending on the quantity of worm castings you need to store, Ziploc bags (with a few air holes punched around the top) are good containers kept in a cool, dark place. Plastic garbage bags with air holes at the top could work for large quantities. The 20% moisture is attained when you take a handful, squeeze it and the mass should just hold together. Any wetter and you'll need to dry it out a bit. If it's drier, simply spritz with a spray bottle or fine-mist from a hose and mix until the squeeze test succeeds. To take the guesswork out, I would suggest investing in a moisture meter. It's not a good idea to store longer than 6 months, certainly no longer than a year and always keeping tabs on the moisture content.

WORM TEA

Joe Urbach summarized the differences between leachate, worm tea, and aerobic compost tea:

Leachate is the correct word for the dark liquid that comes out of the bottom of your worm bin. If your bin is maintained correctly, you should have very little leachate and what you do have can be used safely (in 1:10 diluted form) on your ornamental plants. Sometimes leachate is incorrectly referred to as "worm tea." Some sites refer to it at as "worm wee," but even that is technically incorrect.

Simple Worm Tea a mix of worm castings and water. Useful if you don't have an air pump but still want some liquid fertilizer from your worm bin.

Aerobic Compost Tea an aerated mixture of worm castings, non-chlorinated water, and molasses or another microbial food source. It contains an active culture of microorganisms and should be used immediately, otherwise the benefit of aeration is all but lost. ("Leachate, Worm Tea, and Aerobic Compost Tea: A Clarification," The Grow Network, October 2, 2015)

According to Sierra Worm Composting, "Worm tea is the liquid concentrate of worm compost. Minerals and microbial elements are extracted from the solid compost by actively brewing in water by means of an air pump which forces oxygen into the liquid."

"A primary reason for producing a compost tea is to transfer microbial biomass, fine particulate organic matter, and soluble chemical components of compost into a solution that can be applied to plant surfaces and soils in ways not possible or economically feasible with solid compost." (USDA Compost Tea Task Force Report, April 2004)

Sierra Worm Composting explained:

> While a compost extraction can be made by simply stirring, it's even better if continuous oxygen is incorporated into this "compost broth" that can increase the original numbers of microbes into the billions. This is known as actively aerated compost tea or AACT, in this case, worm tea.
>
> The watery drainage that seeps out of the bottom of a bin is **not** compost tea as many sites assert. Seeping through undigested food waste, this leachate (as it is known) could contain toxic anaerobic microbes that would be harmful to plants. Not only will there be unmineralized organic compounds, but there is the potential for contamination of pathogen organisms and coliform bacteria that can come from some of the raw materials (another reason to always pre-compost fresh manure) put into worm bin systems. The best place for this leachate to go is **back in the bin**. That way, it gets exposed to the worm's gut, to be inoculated with good microbes, and is excreted fully sanitized.
>
> Technically speaking, soaking or steeping compost in a bucket of water is not compost tea. This is termed a liquid compost extract.

> It is beneficial to a certain extent, but you don't get the growth of microbes like in the aerated version. (sierra-worm-compost.com/worm-tea.html)

Here is a non-continuous aeration method adapted from Sierra Worm Composting:

> Fill a used burlap or paint strainer bag with worm compost at the ratio of 1:5 (pounds of compost to gallons of water) and set it in a five- or six-gallon bucket of warm water. Pond or rain water is best, but if using tap water, let it sit an hour (preferably in the sun) to dissipate the chlorine that is antibacterial and antifungal. Process tea for 24 to 48 hours, stirring every couple of hours during the day. (*Organic Farming Research Foundation*, Winter 2001, No. 9)

Kathy and Joel Adams see great results in their garden using "worm juice" to fertilize their plants. Inside their elevated stock tanks, upside down bread crates catch the debris and leave a space for the liquid to fall through, still maintaining a habitat for the worms and preventing them from drowning. They have added spigots to the bottom edges of the bins, with enough elevated space to fit five-gallon buckets. With this method, they have had a great deal of success keeping the moisture level of the worm bins between 70% and 85%. Kathy believes that the worms will die in a moisture level below 50%. They add food scraps and peat moss and monitor the pH level regularly. They keep their bins watered regularly but cover them if rain is forecast. They do not use tap water. The worm juice naturally collects in the base of the stock tank, filling the buckets beneath. To fertilize,

▲ Children love to help tend to the garden. Applying vermicompost and watering are great ways for them to help.

they use two tablespoons of "worm juice" per gallon of water to make a vermicompost tea.

We have had luck steeping a large burlap sack of worm castings in the 200-gallon water tank attached to the waterwheel transplanter. We were able to fertilize with worm tea as we were planting, which really helped the crops.

GARDEN APPLICATIONS

Worm castings are the aggregate dark brown rich soil medium found at the very bottom of the vermicompost bin. In garden applications, they make a nutrient-rich natural fertilizer that helps to boost soil immunity, increase soil fertility, increase plant health and disease resistance, strengthen roots, and improves yields and overall plant health. The following are specific applications for worm castings:

Worm castings and compost can be made into a nutrient-rich compost tea, which can be used to water garden plants. We use one part vermicompost to ten parts water. Simply fill a burlap sack, a potato sack, or any mesh bag with vermicompost. Add it to a large bin, such as a Rubbermaid container or 55-gallon drum and fill with water. Steep the bag for a minimum of one day and a maximum of one week. You may scale this recipe down to make it appropriate to your garden size. Apply when transplanting vegetables, herbs, and fruits.

Results of using both compost and worm castings for plant vitality and growth, as well as building healthy soils, are rewarding. As diversified vegetable growers, we love our compost. It has made an enormous difference on crops such as tomatoes, eggplant, and peppers.

SHARING THE LOVE IN THE COMMUNITY AND THE CLASSROOM

▲ Share the love.

Because worms reproduce regularly and rapidly, you should divide them every four to six months. If the worms are too crowded, there is a good possibility that they will not be getting enough nutrition. They should have enough space to move around and source nutrients. If you think you have too many in one bin, you probably do.

SHARING YOUR WORMS

If you don't plan on starting a worm business, consider sharing your worms, such as giving them away to local gardening clubs, schools, and community gardens. Another idea is to partner with a non-profit gardening organization and apply for a grant to build worm bins and distribute them to local classrooms, community gardens, and farms. I have seen some really cool projects happening on the West Coast where community gardens both compost and vermicompost. On site is a permanent large sifter where residents can drop off compost and remove and sift broken-down compost from a tray underneath the bin. They can then each take a specific amount home to use in their own yard or their community garden plot.

The worms can be sold by the pound to garden enthusiasts at the farmers market or through a website, although regulations may vary state by state. Separate the worms first, weigh them, and then put into breathable bags with some food scraps and bedding to tide them over while they are being transported.

WORM HEALTH

As mentioned in chapter 6, worms thrive in very specific conditions. Temperature, moisture content, adequate food and bedding, and the proper balance of carbon and nitrogen each play a huge role in worm health.

Temperature Buy a thermometer to help regulate the temperature in your worm bin. Small-scale vermicomposters like to keep their worms in the basement versus outside because it is easier to maintain the ideal conditions. If outside, make sure they have adequate shade in the summer and adequate sun in the winter. They will need plenty of moisture and aeration in the summer and plenty of insulation during the winter. Straw bales work best for insulation.

▲ Share your worms with friends, family and fellow gardeners.

Moisture Remember that worms breathe through their skin and must have adequate moisture available as they need it. The ideal moisture level is 70% to 85%. If the bin is too wet, the materials will start to compact at the base, which can lead to an anaerobic environment that is not good for your worm friends and could also lead to a foul odor.

Space Be sure your worms have plenty of square feet to move around in. The wider and shorter the bin, the better. The more space the worms have to move around in a horizontal fashion, the better.

pH Balance You should regularly check the pH balance of your bin. As a general rule, it should stay between 6 and 8. Avoid citrus in your vermicompost bin to prevent any problem. If your pH reads below 6, try adding crushed egg shells or oyster shells. If the pH is still off, try adding a small amount of lime with at least 95% $CaCO_3$. Using the right kind of lime is very important as other types of lime would be harmful to your worms.

Food Remember to feed your worms regularly. They need consistent additions of both carbon and nitrogen materials. Be sure they have plenty of scraps and bedding.

Bedding There are several types of bedding to choose from: coconut coir, shredded newspaper, shredded office paper, strips of cardboard, wood chips (not cedar), fallen leaves, toilet paper rolls, paper towel rolls, paper plates, napkins, and paper towels. There are conflicting opinions as to which types of manure work and which ones to avoid.

SHARING THE KNOWLEDGE IN THE COMMUNITY AND THE CLASSROOM

Vermicomposting is an excellent way to engage in the community, especially when it comes to children and gardening. Vermicomposting helps build healthy soil and fosters a relationship with the soil as a life-giving force.

Vermicomposting can be can be set up and maintained as a fundraiser for a school, gardening club, or community garden. Worms and worm castings can be sold at a farmers market, plant sales, or local garden shops. The potential funds raised by selling worms or vermicompost depends on the amount harvested and collected, the size of the venue, and the number of attendees. Organizations could also start a mail order business, but this method is fairly complicated in terms of maintaining perfect temperature and moisture content while keeping an environment where weed seeds are not viable.

Ideas for Sharing the Knowledge

Information sharing is a powerful tool. Individuals who are passionate about a specific topic that can potentially bring about positive social and environmental change within their communities become catalysts of change. They inspire others to do the same. The actions ripple out into the world, and real change begins to happen in your own community. The more this knowledge is spread, the less we begin to rely on synthetic and dangerous chemical fertilizers. It takes a village!

- Host workshops for friends in your own backyard.
- Lead tours at area vermicompost sites.
- Network with other individuals who keep worms as a hobby and hold monthly meetings at your home or at the library.
- Develop PowerPoint presentations, one for kids and one for adults, about worm farming to present at local schools, gardening clubs, nurseries, community gardens, and farms.
- Start a blog about vermicomposting. Include the basics like bin size, aeration, moisture, food, and bedding but also incorporate lots of pictures, fun facts, videos, charts, graphics, and more.
- Start a YouTube channel on keeping worms as a hobby or vermicomposting in the classroom.
- Set up speaking engagements at the public library with your local master gardeners and master naturalists groups.
- Host vermiculture meetups to share information, worms, favorite books, websites, etc.

INTEGRATING VERMICULTURE INTO SCIENCE CURRICULUM, GRADE 2 TO GRADE 8

Family/classroom/homeschool applications include basic experiments, observations, and activities, as well as worksheets and lessons for incorporating into the science curriculum.

There are many ways to integrate vermiculture into science and outdoor classroom curriculum. As a specialized topic, it may only fit certain core topics in science, such as life in the soil, food production,

or decomposition. However, in the outdoor classroom setting, it can serve as an ongoing part of the curriculum, advancing with each grade.

Lesson One: Life in the Soil

A visiting scientist could give a talk on life in the soil. This peaks the students' interest while hearing the scientist explain their passion for science and why they chose that particular career.

The students take turns viewing multiple soil samples under a microscope and record and draw what they see. The instructor or visiting scientist would then show clear samples in a PowerPoint presentation or from a book, explaining the different organisms, their functions in the soil, and other interesting facts about each microorganism.

Older students could write reports about 12 different microorganisms found in the soil and their functions. They could use vials with lids to collect several soil types from around their home or neighborhood.

Additionally, the instructor could collect several different soil samples by the shovel load and place them in separate boxes. Students would look at the soil, move it around, examine it with a magnifying glass, discover what types of organisms are visible, and hypothesize about the functions of those organisms. Students can record their observations and draw what they see.

Then the instructor would introduce vermiculture and the roles worms play in the soil could be discussed.

Fun fact: "There are more soil microorganisms in a teaspoon of healthy soil than there are people on the Earth!" (nrcs.usda.gov/Internet/FSE_DOCUMENTS/stelprdb1101660.pdf)

Millions of species and billions of organisms — bacteria, algae, microscopic insects, earthworms, beetles, ants, mites, fungi, and more — represent the greatest concentration of biomass anywhere on the planet! Microbes, which make up only one half of one percent of the total soil mass, are the yeasts, algae, protozoa, bacteria, nematodes, and fungi that process organic matter into rich, dark, stable humus in the soil.

Lesson Two: Time-Lapse of Life in the Soil

There are many wonderful videos that provide time-lapse footage of the decomposition process, showing dozens of organisms that are working relentlessly in the soil. The finest I have seen is by Louie

Worms at Work Worm Bin Observation Record

Date worm bin was created _____

Class_____

Type of worms used _____

Number of worms added to bin _____ Worms were sourced from _____

Bedding added_____

_____

Temperature _____ Moisture level _____

Food scraps added _____

Day 1 _____

Day 2 _____

Day 3 _____

Day 4 _____

Day 5 _____

Week One observation summary

_____

_____

_____

Month Two observation summary

_____

_____

_____

Month Three observation summary

_____

_____

Month Four observation summary

_____

_____

Schwartzberg. Gregor Skoberne also made great time-lapse footage of worms moving through various layers of sawdust, soil, and kitchen scraps in a clear education worm bin.

Lesson Three: Worm Anatomy

Students could learn about the physical traits and functions of worms' body parts and how long they take to digest. A large model can be made out of a pool noodle. See homegrownfun.com/model-red-wiggler-worm for a great example!

Lesson Four: Types of Worms

The students can learn that there are more than 7,000 types of worms, but only a few are used in vermicomposting. Teachers can discuss the various types and and their roles in decomposition, and show images of composting worms.

Discussion questions could include:

- Approximately how many types of worms are there?
- Name three varieties that are used in composting.
- Draw a picture of a red wriggler worm.
- Name two roles worms play in decomposition.

Lesson Five: Educational Worm Bins

Over time, students can observe the process of decomposition that takes place with the help of worms. They will witness the lifecycle of a worm. Students can document items placed in the worm bin and in what quantity. They can record how long it takes for bacteria, fungi, worms, and other organisms and microorganisms to break down fruits and vegetables, such as banana peels and apple cores. They can take photos or sketch their observations of the worm bin each week. They can record observations on the worksheet provided.

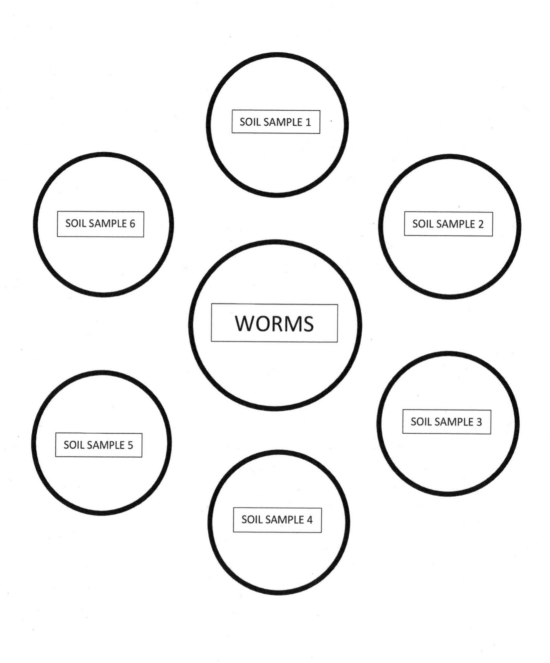

Lesson Six: Sorting and Weighing Worms

In a vermicompost bin, worms multiply rapidly when conditions are optimal. Worms should be separated every six months to prevent overcrowding. This is a good time to share worms with other teachers or move worms to the outdoor compost bin or into the underground pipe worm farm. The children could count how many it takes to equal one pound of worms.

Lesson Seven: Worms and Soil Composition

Students could participate in collecting samples of soil from their backyards or neighborhood parks. With guidance from the instructor, they will place dots, equally spaced, in a circle on a large tarp in the classroom away from direct sunlight, as per the worksheet for this activity. The students put two to three cups of a soil sample on each dot and label it with their name and soil composition. The worms are placed in the middle of the circle and naturally migrate to the soil that attracts them. Students could form hypotheses based on which samples the worms like best and why and fill out the worksheets provided. Are some samples moister than others? Do some contain more organic material? Are some loamy or sandy?

Lesson Eight: Sensitivity to Light

Although worms have no eyes, they are highly sensitive to light. Several activities can be done to demonstrate this. Lesson Seven can be modified and done under a shade tree with the same concept. The students would be observing and recording how quickly the worms get into the piles of soil, away from the light.

GARDEN FIELD DAYS

Garden field days are a great way to introduce vermiculture and vermicomposting. The ideas below are designed for schools or homeschool groups with a garden in place.

Each child receives a stapled packet with ten different simple worksheets for recording observations, drawing pictures, and

◀ Worms and soil composition.

making notes. They will vary for the grade levels and the stations you choose to include in the field day.

Station One: Life in the Soil

Learning objective: Children will learn the living components that make up the soil. They will learn to identify several organisms that can be seen with the naked eye and learn the roles that each play in the soil. They will compare and contrast various soil samples. They will learn basic microscope use while viewing microorganisms in the soil under magnification.

Station supplies Several soil samples in separate boxes, magnifying glasses, portable microscopes, slides and slide covers, tweezers, and several vials of soil samples set up side by side.

Preparation The day before, collect several different soil samples by the shovel load, each to be placed in a separate box.

Station activity Students look at the soil, move it around, use a magnifying glass to discover what types of organisms are visible, and draw hypotheses on the functions of those organisms based on their observations. Students record their observations and draw what they see. An instructor and volunteers assist each child in using a microscope to view microorganisms.

Station Two: Germination

Learning objective Children will learn about seed germination, how much time it requires, the structure and growth of plants.

Station supplies Seeds, seed flats or pots, germination mix, watering can with a shower spout, spray bottle, sunny window, and index cards.

Preparation At least two weeks ahead of time, plant ten different pots or seed flats with various seeds. Seeds that have quick germination include green beans, adzuki beans, pole beans, broccoli, radish, kale, chard, sunflower, squash, and chia. All of the seeds would be given the same amount of sunlight, water, and soil mixture. Multiples should be planted just to be sure that germination is successful before the field day.

Station activity Clearly label all seed flats with the plant name on an index card and attach a seed. The students will record observations in terms of plant height, color, leaf shape, stem shape, etc. This could also present as a classroom science lesson or gardening lesson. Turn this preparation into a sprouting race to get children excited about germination. These seedlings can be transplanted into the school garden beds when they are mature enough.

Station Three: Vermiculture

Learning objective Students will learn about decomposition, the roles worms play in the structure of the soil and food production, the life cycle of the worm, and their diet. They will also learn about vermicomposting and how it is beneficial in soil building. They will learn why vermicompost (worm castings) makes a great natural fertilizer for the garden. Students will have a chance to see the vermicompost bin in progress, watching the worms at work.

Preparation Ideally, a vermicompost bin would already be in place at the school or in the school garden. A compost bin will work fine as long as bedding material (shredded newspaper, strips of cardboard, straw, etc.) is readily available on the field day. Worms can then be added to the compost bin. If not, set up a vermicompost bin that day using worms acquired from a reputable vermiculture source.

Station supplies Red wriggler worms, vermicompost or compost bin, or the supplies to make one (see chapter 5).

Station activity Students will look at worm cocoons under a magnifying glass and compare the various sizes of worms during their life cycle. The students will learn through graphs and charts what does and does not go into a vermicompost bin and they will learn what other types of organisms and microorganisms are present in a vermicompost bin. They will learn what worms eat and how they turn food scraps into worm castings with the help of their anatomy and microorganisms.

Station Four: Planting

Learning objective Children will learn about proper planting methods, light and spacing requirements, germination mixes, seed germination time, and care and transplanting of seedlings.

Preparation Gather supplies and set up on a table. Choose the right seeds depending on the time of year.

Station supplies Seeds (green beans, marigolds, basil, and sunflowers have good germination rates), a shallow bin full of germination mix, more bags of mix to refill, pots, plant labels, and markers or pencils, a watering can or spray bottle, a photo of the plant that matches the corresponding seed.

Station activity With help from instructors, students will fill their pot with germination mix, plant seeds of their choice, spray with water, and make a label with their name and the seed variety.

This activity is best when the pots are left to sprout in the classroom, allowing students to monitor the plants daily and can keep a record, furthering their participation in this lesson. The pots can be separated by varieties. Possible activities for the continued lesson include a sprouting race to see which seeds germinates fastest, sprouting chart, seedling measurements, etc.

Station Five:
Weeding and Garden Maintenance

Learning objective Students will learn about weeds and various ways to remove them from the garden. They will be able to identify four common weeds and how to use them as compost material, green manure, or food for humans (such as dandelions and lamb's quarters). Students will learn the life cycles of specific weeds and how to pull them before they go to seed, to prevent more weeds.

Preparation Laminate a few examples of weeds onto plain paper and label them to show students which ones they will be pulling. Have tools and gloves ready and near area they will be working. Weed a small plot of the garden to show an example of what a weeded garden bed should look like.

Station supplies Hand weeding tools, gloves, examples of weeds students should pull (either fresh, laminated, or photos of weeds present in the garden).

Station activity Instructors and volunteers will carefully supervise students in pulling weeds in a specific area of the garden bed. They can either lay the weeds in piles or the instructor can show them how to utilize the weeds as green manure as long as they haven't gone to seed.

Station Six:
Harvesting and Processing

Learning objective Students will learn how to properly harvest and wash produce. They will also learn how to store the produce to keep it fresh.

Preparation Have supplies ready and near harvesting area. Prepare a washtub full of water.

Station supplies Buckets or bins to hold harvested material, a large tub filled with water for washing produce.

Station activity Instructors and volunteers carefully supervise students in harvesting ripe produce in the school garden.

Station Seven:
Seed Saving

Learning objective Students will learn the miraculous ability for one single seed to produce a vegetable with upwards of one hundred seeds and that each of those seeds are capable of yielding several dozen plants, each capable of producing multiple fruits and vegetables that contain the seeds capable of producing several dozen plants! Children will learn the proper seed saving techniques for many different fruits and vegetables.

Preparation Harvest several different varieties of fruits and vegetables from the school garden (or buy organic fruits and vegetables if the timing is not right).

Station supplies Coffee filters, paper plates, paper bags, markers, and other supplies needed for seed saving.

Station activity Instructors will carefully cut open various fruits and vegetables to demonstrate what the different seeds look like. With guidance from volunteers, students will take turns picking the seeds out and separating them from the flesh of the fruits and vegetables. Each variety of seeds will then be placed on a different paper plate or paper bag that is clearly labeled. This activity is typically specific to saving heirloom seeds. Some GMO seeds cannot be regrown. Choose organic, and when possible, heirloom varieties that are homegrown or sourced from a local farmer.

Station Eight: Sample Tasting

Learning objective To get children excited about tasting the flavor complexities and textures of a variety of fruits and vegetables grown in their school garden.

Preparation Have all supplies on hand. Cut and prepare additional samples of fruits and vegetables as backup. Set up next to seed saving station to utilize cut fruits and vegetables. If desired, have a variety of dips on hand to make sampling more fun.

Station supplies Vinyl gloves for serving, platters and tongs, dips in small containers, small compostable paper plates and cups, napkins, and drinking water.

Station activity Allow children to sample a variety of fresh raw fruits and vegetables to experience their unique flavors.

Station Nine: Chef's Choice

Learning objective To introduce students to the farm-to-table culinary arts, to give them a wonderful example of the deliciousness that can be achieved when cooking with in-season produce.

Preparation Contact a chef in your area or the local Slow Foods chapter to get names of chefs who enjoy participating in farm-to-school events.

Station supplies Pop-up kitchen supplies (most chefs will have these) including pots, pans, cooking utensils, towels, water, washing station, hand washing station, electric burner, cutting boards, knives, small mixing bowls, sample cups, etc.

Station activity The students will watch the chef give a quick cooking demonstration on preparing nutritious and delicious snacks and side dishes. The chef will then allow the students to sample each of the creations.

Recap and Quiz

The students can put their knowledge to the test by answering questions as a fun trivia game or through individual quizzes. This will bring the knowledge full circle and allow the students to really retain the information they learned during the field day.

OTHER CURRICULUM APPLICATIONS

This field day learning curriculum could be applied to an eco-friendly field day or green fair, including the following nine topics.

Litter Cleanup

Instructors and volunteers could lead students on a school grounds litter cleanup. At the end, they could place all of their findings on a large tarp and spend time sorting the litter, based on the methods below.

Trash Sorting

Students could sort the various items that travel through the waste system, determining which single-use items could be banned and why and which items could be reduced and reused.

They could separate waste materials into the following categories: reduce, reuse, re-gift, recycle, compost, vermicompost, and finally items for the landfill.

Water Conservation

Students could learn various methods of water conservation, including rainwater catchment, rain gardening, gray water systems, terraced gardening, hugelkultur, swales, and berms.

Alternative Energy

A local solar energy company could come and demonstrate how solar energy works. A local car company could come and give test drives to students and parents or just demonstrate the mechanics of an electric car.

Green Building

A local green building company could come and demonstrate some simple green building methods, such as cob and cordwood.

Gardening

Demonstrations could be given on planting, transplanting, harvesting, seed saving, etc.

Composting

Students could learn how to build a simple compost bin, the benefits of composting, and why it is important. With guidance, they could sort food waste into compost bins.

Vermicomposting

Students could learn the basics of vermiculture, the do's and don'ts of a vermicompost bin, and the life cycle of red wriggler worms.

Soil Conservation

Students could learn why soil conservation is crucial to the future of the planet. They could look at rich healthy soil samples and poor soil samples from elsewhere through university extension programs or requesting samples from agronomists in other countries. The objective would be to learn what components make up healthy soil versus what causes soil degradation.

CONCLUSION

There is a dire need to change the way we as the human race treat the soil, air, and water. There is a dire need to change the way food is produced worldwide. Think of the possibilities if everyone played some part in growing their own food or helping to grow food for their communities. Imagine a neighborhood where one family kept chickens, the next kept bees, someone kept worms, and a few more focused on fruits, vegetables, and herbs. They could can and preserve the harvest together, share weekly meals. They could all share the end bounty and start making steps toward a brighter, more self-reliant future.

While there are many realistic factors that would prevent someone from growing their own food — poverty, homelessness, the aftermath of war — gardens bring communities together and build a foundation for hope. Community gardening projects are sprouting up all over the world. People are uniting through our common need for survival — food. Homeless shelters are receiving donations from local farms; more and more schools are integrating onsite gardens and farm-to-table meal plans for children; prisons worldwide are starting onsite farms and giving prisoners extended outside time and hands-on learning opportunities. The world needs more people growing their own food and teaching others how to grow their own food. The world needs more and more groups, organizations, and individuals working to rebuild healthy soils.

Unless each of us honestly acknowledges and assesses the negative impact we have on the Earth and actually puts solutions-based thinking into practice, we cannot change the future of our home, planet Earth. Understanding that the soil is a living organism covering the Earth, we then can examine and implement simple solutions in the ways we eat and live that everyone can take part in. It could be as simple as planting more trees or creating an organic garden with native pollinator-attracting plants. It could be as simple as removing a few items from your diet that contribute to soil degradation. It could be as simple as shopping locally or joining a CSA farm. It could be as simple as taking public transportation. It could be as simple as buying less unnecessary stuff.

The soil is being destroyed at unprecedented rates by over-consumption, big business, human development, deforestation, monoculture, genetically modified foods, ground water contamination, reliance on fossil fuels, non-sustainable extraction of all of our natural resources, and use of pesticides, herbicides, and fungicides. All of these problems are symptoms of a deeper root cause: our massive disconnect from the earth. The soil is the direct source of a significant amount of nutrients. We need the soil as much as we need the air, but yet only a small percentage of people who care about these issues actually take action to amend them. According to a survey conducted in 2013 by the Pew Research Center, 52% of Americans named protecting the environment as a top priority for Congress, whereas 86% named strengthening the nation's economy as a top priority. Perhaps it's for those 86% that this Cree Indian Prophecy was written: "Only after the last tree has been cut down. Only after the last river has been poisoned. Only after the last fish has been caught. Only then will you find that money cannot be eaten."

Anyone who has ever grown their own food or watched documentaries about food knows that this monoculture-based society not only is unsustainable, but is actually causing irreversible damage to the Earth every day. Despite this, we continue to support these practices, albeit sometimes unintentionally and out of convenience, whether buying prepared meals wrapped in unnecessary packaging or simply buying conventionally grown vegetables at the grocery store. Corn and soy are the crops with the most devastating contribution to monoculture. Unfortunately corn, soy, and wheat are found in the majority of processed foods, especially in the United States.

Of course there are many practices that cause oftentimes irreversible soil degradation: fracking (hydraulic fracturing), oil drilling, mining, strip mining, deforestation, and clear-cutting. Our reliance on fossil fuels is not helping. The simple acts of buying gasoline or using nonrenewable paper, unbeknownst to many, are also contributing to environmental degradation. Access to environmentally friendly everyday products such as paper goods is very limited and often more expensive, making it impossible for those of us on a tight budget to choose to support the companies making a difference. And then there is air and water pollution. It is very hard to witness giant smokestacks lined up along major rivers that were clean and clear less than a century ago. I heard someone say over a decade ago that all of the oceans, rivers, and streams are polluted beyond restoration. This news was devastating. How could humans, in less than 100 years, destroy the water supply around the world? How can we as a human race do our part to change the gloomy future of this planet? When an individual starts to brainstorm solutions, they seem practical and attainable considering the technology that is available.

For instance, what if big companies, factories, and corporations simply stopped producing anything made from nonrenewable resources and instead made the same items from renewable resources such as agricultural waste, hemp, and bamboo and transitioned into powering their factories with renewable energy? Think of the positive impact that would make. Or on a larger scale, what if all the energy giants trained their current employees to operate energy plants using solar and wind power? What if all of the coal-fired power plants and nuclear power plants simply just converted to renewable energy? What if car companies were required by law to stop making gas-powered cars and instead only made either hybrid or solar electric cars? The technology is available.

There are many solutions to these problems. However, each set of solutions has its own problems and unknown ramifications. So where does that leave us? When having this conversation with a dear friend and longtime environmental activist, Jim Scheff, his answer was, "We just need to use less." This is such a simple yet profound insight and is attainable with a little grunt work. To be an example to friends and family members in our own communities and to share our stories big and small will send out ripples within our regions. There are plenty of individual solutions one could implement as well, that almost always have direct impact on other solutions. The solution that I have adopted is food: how it can help heal our bodies, and how it can help heal the Earth. Food is the basic necessity for survival. If everyone in the world knew how to grow their own food, that would reduce our reliance on large-scale industrialized agrarian production, ultimately reducing the need for fossil fuels, chemical applications, and so much more. Food throughout communities would then become localized.

Information sharing is a powerful tool. Individuals who are passionate about a specific topic that has potential to bring about positive social and environmental change within their communities become catalysts of change. They inspire others to do the same. The actions ripple out into the world and real change begins to happen in your own community. The more this knowledge is spread, the less we begin to rely on synthetic and dangerous chemical fertilizers. It takes a village!

ABOUT
THE AUTHOR

CRYSTAL STEVENS is the author of Grow Create Inspire. She is an herbalist, writer, artist and vegetable farmer, employing multiple platforms to share her passion for inspiring others to care for the environment, to grow gardens, and to live healthy lifestyles. Crystal also writes and illustrates children's books. She recently illustrated *Semore the Bird Tells All that he Heard* by Kelley Powers.

She teaches dozens of workshops each year on gardening, composting, vennicomposting, healthy eating, natural living, medicinal herbs and ethical foraging. She also gives presentations at Mother Earth News Fairs around the country. Crystal co-managed La Vista CSA Farm with her husband, Eric, for 7 years. They currently work at EarthDance Organic Farm School in Ferguson Missouri and tend a permaculture inspired micro-farm with their children at their home along the bluffs of the Mississippi River in western) Illinois.

A NOTE ABOUT THE PUBLISHER

New Society Publishers is an activist, solutions-oriented publisher focused on publishing books for a world of change. Our books offer tips, tools, and insights from leading experts in sustainable building, homesteading, climate change, environment, conscientious commerce, renewable energy, and more — positive solutions for troubled times.

We're proud to hold to the highest environmental and social standards of any publisher in North America. This is why some of our books might cost a little more. We think it's worth it!

- We print all our books in North America, never overseas
- All our books are printed on 100% post-consumer recycled paper, processed chlorine free, with low-VOC vegetable-based inks (since 2002)
- Our corporate structure is an innovative employee shareholder agreement, so we're one-third employee-owned (since 2015)
- We're carbon-neutral (since 2006)
- We're certified as a B Corporation (since 2016)

At New Society Publishers, we care deeply about *what* we publish — but also about *how* we do business.

www.newsociety.com

New Society Publishers
ENVIRONMENTAL BENEFITS STATEMENT

For every 5,000 books printed, New Society saves the following resources:[1]

30	Trees
2,695	Pounds of Solid Waste
2,965	Gallons of Water
3,867	Kilowatt Hours of Electricity
4,899	Pounds of Greenhouse Gases
12	Pounds of HAPs, VOCs, and AOX Combined
7	Cubic Yards of Landfill Space

[1]Environmental benefits are calculated based on research done by the Environmental Defense Fund and other members of the Paper Task Force who study the environmental impacts of the paper industry.